B,11

Liturgical Year
or
Little Little Organ Book

Elementary
HARMONY

Elementary

HARMONY

*Theory
and
Practice*

ROBERT W. OTTMAN
*Professor of Music
North Texas State University*

PRENTICE-HALL, INC.   ENGLEWOOD CLIFFS, N.J.

Preface

Elementary Harmony: Theory and Practice and its companion volume, *Advanced Harmony: Theory and Practice* are designed to meet the needs of college courses in basic music theory. Although harmony is still the basic subject in the college music theory curriculum, the trend has been toward greater emphasis upon related skills in ear training, sight singing, and keyboard harmony. This trend has brought about two distinct methods of class organization: the "correlated" class (often called "integrated") in which all these skills are taught by one instructor in one class, and the "non-correlated" class in which the skills are taught in separate classes by one or more instructors. These texts may be used advantageously in either type of organization.

Each chapter is divided into two principal sections. The first, "Theory and Analysis," presents a general theoretical discussion of the subject of the chapter heading, together with projects in analysis from music scores. The second, "Application," is itself divided into three sections: "Written Materials," containing such projects as part-writing, melody harmonization, and original composition; "Ear Training and Reading," containing projects in harmonic, rhythmic, and melodic ear training, and correlation with the author's *Music for Sight Singing* (Englewood Cliffs, N.J.: Prentice-Hall, Inc., 1956); and "Keyboard Harmony," including the playing of the materials of the chapter in abstract exercises, in realization of figured basses, and in melody harmonization.

The texts are based on the techniques of composers of the seventeenth to nineteenth centuries. They include a comprehensive survey of the harmonic materials used in these historical periods, from the simple triad through seventh chords, altered chords, ninth, eleventh, and thirteenth chords, and simple and complex methods of modulation.

The historical limitation in no way implies that teaching of music theory must be limited to this period. But for the undergraduate student, knowledge of the practices of the seventeenth and nineteenth centuries should serve as a point of departure for his study of both pre-seventeenth century music and twentieth century music.

In addition to the theoretical presentation, a comprehensive practical application of these harmonic materials is presented. Concurrent studies in melodic and rhythmic analysis and composition, in harmonic analysis, in instrumentation, and in analysis of form (small forms only) implement this application. With these materials, the student is not only asked to solve traditional figured bass exercises, but is led ultimately to accomplishments in arranging given melodies and in creating original music, in both vocal and instrumental styles. Ample material is given for student work, allowing considerable latitude in choice of assignments. There are several other features which may be of particular interest.

Rudiments. A comprehensive review of the rudiments of music is furnished, so that members of a beginning class in college music theory will be able to find a common starting point.

Part-Writing. The principles of part-writing are codified, making possible easy reference to any part-writing procedure. (See Appendix 1.)

Musical Examples. Hundreds of examples covering a wide range of composers, nationalities, and periods are presented. Examples early in the course are principally in four-part vocal structure. As the text advances, more of the examples are in instrumental style.

Terminology. Unfortunately, there is no standard terminology in music theory. Students often complete a theory course or even attain a degree in music but are unable to understand many articles in the literature of music theory or musicology. This text lists and describes at appropriate places the more important of these varying terminologies.

The method of identification of chords by Roman numeral, explained in Chapter 2 and at appropriate places in later chapters, has been chosen as a compromise between the simplest possible system of identification and the one that is most effective pedagogically, especially in the teaching and learning of techniques in ear training. Each of the many terminologies has its own advantages in differing musical situations. The instructor should feel free to substitute terminologies of his choice whenever they are pedagogically advantageous.

Self-Help in Ear Training. Most chapters contain projects in self-help in ear training, enabling the student to work on this vital aspect of his theoretical training outside of class.

Assignments and Exercises. Material for student participation is divided into "Assignments"—that which can be committed to paper—and "Exercises"—that which can be demonstrated only by speaking or singing or at the keyboard. Both assignments and exercises are numbered consecutively throughout each volume.

Supplementary Materials. Assignments in sight singing and in melodic analysis and melody harmonization are made from the author's *Music for Sight Singing.* Many references besides those illustrated are made to the collection of 371 Chorales by Johann Sebastian Bach; also, a number of assignments in harmonic and melodic analysis are made from this collection.

In appropriate places throughout both volumes, assignments in harmonic analysis are made from these five additional collections of music: Beethoven, Sonatas for Piano (numbers 1-12 only); Chopin, Mazurkas; Mendelssohn, *Songs Without Words;* Mozart, Sonatas for Piano; and Schumann, *Album for the Young,* Op. 68. Many students will already own some or all of these.

All the procedures and materials in these texts have been tested for many years through use in the music theory courses at North Texas State University. The author acknowledges his indebtedness to the many hundreds of undergraduate and graduate students whose participation in the presentation and study of these materials has made the final form of the text possible. Particular thanks are due the members of the NTSU theory faculty, Frank Mainous, Alan Richardson, and William Gardner, for their cooperation in teaching these materials on an experimental basis and for their many able suggestions and constructive criticisms resulting from this classroom experience.

ROBERT W. OTTMAN

ANALYTICAL TABLE OF CONTENTS

Chapter	Theory and Analysis				Written Materials					Ear Training and Music Reading						Keyboard Harmony	
	Theory	Melodic Analysis	Form Analysis	Harmonic Analysis	Chord Studies	Melody Writing	Part-Writing	Melody Harmonization	Original Composition	Chord Studies	Melodic Dictation	Rhythmic Dictation	Harmonic Dictation	Rhythmic Reading	Sight Singing	Chord Studies	Melody Harmonization
1. Rudiments	1																
2. Major Triad	15	18			18					20	25					26	
3. Rhythm (I) (Division of the Beat)	27											38		36			
4. Melodic Line (I) (Form: Phrase and Period)	40	43	43			44			44		47				46	48	
5. Connection of Chords	49						52										
6. Minor Triad	58	60			63	63	63		63	65	67				67	67	
7. Tonic and Dominant Harmonies	68	71		70		73	74		73	77	79		78		79	79	80
8. Alto and Tenor Clefs	81										84				84		

No.	Topic	Pages
11.	Triad in Inversion	105, 108, 119, 121, 123, 125, 125
12.	Rhythm (II) (Subdivision of the Beat)	122, 144, 144
13.	Non-Harmonic Tones (I)	126, 134
14.	Leading Tone Triad	148, 151, 152, 153, 156, 160, 161, 162, 163
15.	Supertonic Triad	164, 166, 166, 171, 175, 175, 176, 176
16.	Melodic Line (II) (Form: Phrase Group, Double Period, Extensions)	178, 183, 183, 183, 183, 184, 185
17.	Submediant Triad	186, 191, 191, 203, 205
	Mediant Triad	188, 191, 197, 201, 203, 203, 204, 205, 206
18.	Miscellaneous Triad Usages	208, 212, 220, 221, 221, 221
19.	Non-Harmonic Tones (II)	222, 236, 243, 246, 246, 246, 246, 247
20.	Dominant Seventh Chord	248, 251, 253, 266, 266
	Supertonic Seventh	252, 252, 258, 260, 264, 264, 264, 266, 266
	Syncopation	265, 264, 266, 266

Contents

1

THE FUNDAMENTALS OF
MUSIC THEORY: A REVIEW, 1

2

THE MAJOR TRIAD, 15

3

RHYTHM (I), 27

4

THE MELODIC LINE (I), 40

5

THE CONNECTION OF CHORDS, 49

6

THE MINOR TRIAD;
THE MELODIC LINE IN MINOR, 58

7

THE THREE PRINCIPAL
TRIADS OF THE KEY;
TONIC AND DOMINANT HARMONIES, 68

8

THE ALTO AND
TENOR CLEFS, 81

9

THE SUBDOMINANT TRIAD;
PLAGAL CADENCES, 85

10

FURTHER USE OF
THE THREE PRINCIPAL TRIADS, 91

11

THE TRIAD
IN INVERSION, 105

12

RHYTHM:
SUBDIVISION OF THE BEAT, 122

13

NON-HARMONIC TONES (I), 126

14

THE LEADING
TONE TRIAD, 148

15

THE SUPERTONIC TRIAD, 164

16

THE MELODIC LINE (II), 178

17

THE SUBMEDIANT
AND MEDIANT TRIADS, 186

18

MISCELLANEOUS
TRIAD USAGES, 208

19

NON-HARMONIC TONES (II), 222

20

INTRODUCTION TO
DIATONIC SEVENTH CHORDS;
RHYTHM: SYNCOPATION, 248

Appendix 1

THE ESSENTIALS OF
PART-WRITING, 268

Appendix 2

INSTRUMENTATION:
RANGES, CLEFS,
TRANSPOSITION, 272

INDEX, 279

Elementary

HARMONY

The Fundamentals of
Music Theory: A Review

The material of this chapter is prerequisite to the study of music theory as presented in the following chapters. A thorough review of these fundamentals is advisable before beginning work in Chapter 2.

PITCH

1. PITCH NAMES. Pitches are named with the first seven letters of the alphabet, A B C D E F G.

2. STAFF. The staff (plural, *staves*) consists of five lines and four spaces.

3. G CLEF   . When placed on the staff, the line encircled by the lower loop of the clef sign is designated G. This clef sign is commonly used to designate the second line as G, and in this position it is known as a *treble clef*.

4. F CLEF   . When placed on the staff, the line between the dots is designated F. This clef commonly designates the fourth line as F, and in this position it is known as a *bass clef*.

5. STAFF SPELLINGS. Adjacent lines and spaces use adjacent pitch names from the alphabet.

6. LEGER (LEDGER) LINES AND SPACES. Leger lines are short lines written above or below the staff for the purpose of extending the staff. Spaces between leger lines are leger spaces.

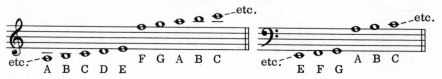

7. GREAT STAFF (GRAND STAFF). The treble and bass clefs joined together constitute the great staff.

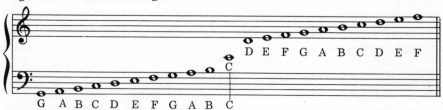

8. HALF STEPS AND WHOLE STEPS. Two pitches from the musical alphabet or from the piano keyboard as close together as possible constitute a half step. In the musical alphabet, E-F and B-C are half steps, since no pitch sound is found between them. Other adjacent pairs of letter names are whole steps (two half steps). On the keyboard, any two adjacent keys sound a half step.

9. CHROMATICS

A *sharp* (♯) raises the pitch of a note one half step. (C♯ is one half step higher than C.)

A *flat* (♭) lowers the pitch of a note one half step.

A *double sharp* (✕) raises the pitch of a note a whole step.

A *double flat* (♭♭) lowers the pitch of a note a whole step.

A *natural* (♮) cancels out a previously used chromatic.

The relative pitch relationships of the chromatics are

(low) ♭♭   ♭   ♮   ♯   ✕ (high)

10. THE KEYBOARD. Names of the keys on the piano can be seen in the figure below.

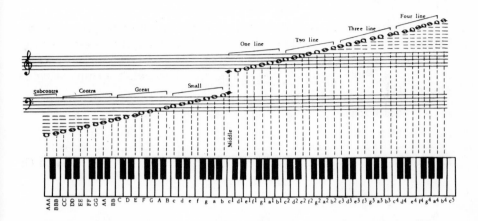

Courtesy of Raymond Elliott, *Fundamentals of
Music* (Englewood Cliffs, N.J.: Prentice-
Hall, Inc., 1955).

11. OCTAVE REGISTERS. This is a system in which identical pitch names in various octave positions may be differentiated from each other. Middle C is designated C^1 (read "one-line C"). Each pitch is designated in the figure above. (For other systems of pitch differentiation, see "Pitch names" in *Harvard Dictionary of Music*.)

12. SCALES. A scale is a series of pitches using, in order, the seven letter names of the musical alphabet, beginning on any one letter.

Major scale. A series of eight tones (8 being the pitch-name repetition of 1) in which the relationship between successive tones is as follows (1 = whole step, 1/2 = half step):

Scale tones	1	2	3	4	5	6	7	8
Step size		1	1	1/2	1	1	1	1/2

Using C on the keyboard as 1, the major scale makes use of the white keys exclusively.

When beginning the major scale on any other letter name, it is necessary to add chromatics to maintain the relationship of half steps and whole steps.

Minor scales. A series of eight tones in which the relationship between successive tones differs from that of the major scale. There are three forms of minor scales.

   a) *Pure (natural) minor scale.* The relationship between successive tones is as follows:

Scale tones	1		2		3		4		5		6		7		8
Step size		1		1/2		1		1		1/2		1		1	

Examples of the pure minor scale starting on A (no chromatics) and G:

   b) *Harmonic minor scale.* The harmonic form of the minor scale is similar to the pure form, with the seventh scale degree raised one half step. This results in a distance of 1 1/2 steps between 6 and 7 and a half step between 7 and 8.

   c) *Melodic minor scale.* Ascending only, the melodic form of the minor scale is similar to the pure form with the sixth and seventh degrees each raised one half step.

   The descending form of the melodic minor scale is identical to that of the pure minor scale.

8	7	6	5	4	3	2	1
A	G	F	E	D	C	B	A

Chromatic scale. A scale consisting exclusively of half steps.

C C# D D# E F F# G G# A A# B C   ascending

C B B♭ A A♭ G G♭ F E E♭ D D♭ C   descending

13. SCALE DEGREE NAMES

Scale degree	Name: *major key*	Scale degree	Name: *minor key*
1	Tonic	1	Tonic
2	Supertonic	2	Supertonic
3	Mediant	3	Mediant
4	Subdominant	4	Subdominant
5	Dominant	5	Dominant
6	Submediant	6	Submediant
7	Leading tone	♯6	Raised submediant
		7	Subtonic
		♯7	Leading tone

(♯6 and ♯7 mean raised sixth scale step and raised seventh scale step.)

14. INTERVALS. An interval is the distance between two pitches. It can be measured by the number of half steps and/or whole steps it contains and then identified by an interval name.

Intervals are named according to the number of letter names encompassed in the interval. For example, C up to F is a *fourth* since four letter names (C, D, E and F) are encompassed. Interval names are qualified by the terms *major, minor, perfect, diminished,* and *augmented.* Major, minor, and perfect intervals above C are

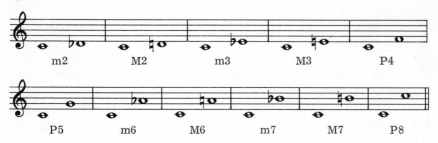

m2—minor second, a half step.
M2—major second, a whole step.
m3—minor third, a whole step plus a half step (three half steps).[1]

---

[1]Not to be confused with the interval between the sixth and seventh scale steps of the harmonic minor scale. This latter interval also consists of a whole step plus a half step, but encompasses only two letter names, and is therefore called an *augmented second.* Intervals which sound the same but are spelled and named differently are known as *enharmonic* intervals. The term *enharmonic* also applies to pairs of single pitches (C♯-D♭) or pairs of chords (F♯ A♯ C♯ - G♭ B♭ D♭) which sound the same but are spelled differently.

M3—major third, two whole steps (four half steps).
P4—perfect fourth, two whole steps plus one half step (five half steps).
P5—perfect fifth, a major third plus a minor third (seven half steps).
m6—minor sixth, a perfect fifth plus a half step (eight half steps).
M6—major sixth, a perfect fifth plus a whole step (nine half steps).
m7—minor seventh, an octave less one whole step (ten half steps).
M7—major seventh, an octave less one half step (eleven half steps) .
P8—perfect octave, two pitches with the same name separated by twelve half
   steps.

Minor intervals are one half step smaller than major intervals. Diminished intervals are one half step smaller than minor or perfect intervals (e.g., C up to F♭, diminished fourth). Augmented intervals are one half step larger than major or perfect intervals (for example, C up to A♯, augmented sixth).

In addition, there are two other intervals, the *perfect prime* (PP), no distance between pitches, and the augmented prime (AP), a half step in which both pitches use the same letter name.

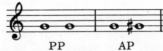

   PP   AP

15. INVERSION OF INTERVALS. Intervals may be inverted by placing the lower note one octave higher, or the higher note one octave lower. In this process, major intervals invert to minor intervals, and minor intervals invert to major intervals. Perfect intervals remain perfect when inverted, hence their name.

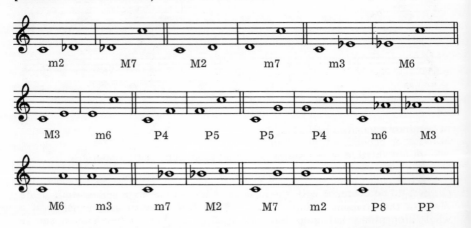

16. KEY AND KEY SIGNATURE. A key signature is a grouping of those chromatics found in the scale and placed on the staff immediately after the clef sign. For example, from the E major scale shown

in the discussion of the major scale, the four sharps may be extracted and placed on the staff.

These chromatics ordinarily need not appear thereafter in the musical composition.   For minor key signatures, chromatics from the pure minor scale are used.   The pure minor scale on C♯ also has four sharps.

In music of the seventeenth to nineteenth centuries, the key signature is commonly used to identify the tonic note of the scale used at the beginning and end of the composition.   Thus a signature of four sharps will indicate to the performer that the tonic note is either E of the E major scale, or C♯ of the C♯ minor scale.

A given piece is said to be in a certain *key,* the name of which is identical with the letter name of the tonic note of the scale.   These are the key signatures, together with their tonic notes and names.

Major keys

Minor keys

In the bass clef, the chromatics of the key signature are arranged as follows:

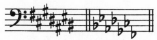

Relative keys.   Two keys, each using the same key signature, are known as relative keys, for example, G major (1 sharp) and E minor (1 sharp).

Parallel keys. Two keys, each using the same letter name for tonic note, are known as parallel keys, e.g., G major and G minor.

17. CIRCLE OF KEYS. Keys whose tonic notes are located at the interval of a perfect fifth (or its inversion, the perfect fourth) from each other will show one chromatic difference in their key signatures. Upon this principle, all keys may be shown in a circle of keys.

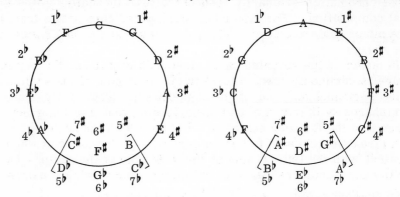

(Key names located within brackets are enharmonic keys.)

18. CHORD. A chord is a group of different notes, usually three or more, sounded simultaneously or in rapid succession *(broken chord)*. Chords in the music of the seventeenth to nineteenth centuries are ordinarily found spelled in thirds, for example, C E G, D F♯ A C, and so on.

19. TRIAD. A three-note chord spelled in thirds is called a triad. Triads may be constructed from any combination of major and minor thirds. Four such combinations are possible.

- *c*) two minor thirds: diminished triad
- *b*) two major thirds: augmented triad
- *c*) one major third and one minor third, in that order from the lowest note up: major triad.
- *d*) one minor third and one major third, in that order from the lowest note up: minor triad.

DURATION

20. NOTES AND RESTS. Durations of pitch or silence are indicated, in part, by characteristic note-shapes or rest signs.

Double whole note	‖o‖	Double whole rest	
Whole Note	o	Whole Rest	
Half Note	♩	Half Rest	
Quarter Note	♩	Quarter Rest	⸓ or ↾
Eighth Note	♪	Eighth Rest	𝄾
Sixteenth Note	♪	Sixteenth Rest	𝄿
Thirty-Second Note	♪	Thirty-Second Rest	𝅀
Sixty-Fourth Note	♪	Sixty-Fourth Rest	𝅁

The whole rest is also used to indicate a complete measure rest regardless of the number of beats in the measure.

These note-shapes do not indicate actual duration of time until combined with a tempo indication and a time signature (see below). They do indicate relative relationships of duration as expressed by their names.   For example, a whole note (or rest) is equal in duration to two half notes (or rests) or to four quarter notes.   Any note value is equal in duration to two notes of the next smaller value.

21. BEAT.   A beat is a unit of musical time. It can be represented visibly by the movement of a conductor's hand, or audibly by the ticking sound of a metronome. A beat may be represented on the staff by any note value indicated above. (See also "dot" and "time signature" below.)

22. BAR. This is a vertical line appearing on the staff (sometimes called "bar-line").

23. DOUBLE BAR. Two vertical lines on the staff at the close of a composition or a major division of a composition are called a double bar.

24. MEASURE.   A measure is a group of notes or rests found between two bars (bar-lines). Usually each measure represents a fixed number of beats as indicated by the time signature (see below). The word "bar" is often used to mean "measure."

25. DOT.   A dot appearing after a note or rest, for example, ♩•, increases the value of the note by one half: ♩• = ♩ + ♪. A dotted note or rest is equal in value to three notes of the next smaller value: ♩• = ♩♩♩, ♪. = ♪♪♪, —• = ¿ ¿ ¿. Any dotted note can be used to represent the beat.

26. TIE.   A curved line joining two successive notes of identical pitch is a tie. The two tied notes sound as one note. ♩ ♩ = 𝅗𝅥

27. TEMPO. Tempo is the rate of speed of a composition. It may be expressed at the beginning of a composition or during a composition by musical terms such as *allegro* or *adagio* or by a metronome marking such as ♩ = 60 M.M. (M.M. is Maelzel's Metronome). "60" on the metronome indicates one tick per second. The marking ♩ = 60 means that the duration of each quarter note will be one second.

28. TIME SIGNATURE. The time signature consists of two Arabic numerals, arranged vertically, found at the beginning of a musical composition following the clef and the key signature.

In its simplest definition, the upper number of the time signature states the number of beats to be found in each measure, while the lower number indicates which of the possible note values will receive one beat.

$\frac{2}{4}$, two beats in a measure, a quarter note receives one beat.

$\frac{3}{8}$, three beats in a measure, an eighth note receives one beat.

Very often, certain time signatures in certain situations will convey other meanings. In a slow tempo, $\frac{6}{8}$ may be interpreted as above, but in a fast tempo it invariably indicates two beats in a measure with a ♩. note receiving one beat (two ♩. = six ♪ notes). In any case, the upper number always indicates how many of the note values expressed by the lower number will be found in one measure. Clarification of this situation will be found in Chapter 3.

Although the time signature can be made up of many combinations of two numbers, these are the most often used.

> Upper number: 2, 3, 4, 6, 9, 12
>
> Lower number: 2, 4, 8, 16

The sign **C** (often called *common time*) is a substitute for $\frac{4}{4}$.

The sign **¢** (often called *cut time* or *alla breve*) is a substitute for $\frac{2}{2}$.

ELEMENTARY NOTATION

29. THE SINGLE NOTE.   A note is drawn with one, two or three parts:

    ○   head   ♩ stem   ♪ flag

An ascending stem is found on the right side of the head (♩).

A descending stem is found on the left side of the head (♩).

30. NOTES ON THE STAFF.   *a)* When writing notes for a single part (one voice or one instrument) on the staff, place descending stems on notes found on the middle line or above, and ascending stems on notes below the middle line.

When the note on the middle line is the highest note of the measure, it is often found with an ascending stem.

b) When writing for two parts on a single staff, notes for the upper part use ascending stems and notes for the lower part use descending stems, regardless of their location on the staff.

c) To indicate two parts performing the same pitch on a single staff (unisons), use a single note head with both ascending and descending stems. For two whole notes in unison, use two overlapping whole notes.

31. NOTES USING LEGER LINES OR SPACES. Above the staff, do not write leger lines above the highest note. Below the staff, do not write leger lines below the lowest note.

32. DOTTED NOTES. When the note head is on a space, the dot is found in the same space. When the note is on a line, the dot is usually found in the space above, though it is sometimes in the space below.

33. VERTICAL ARRANGEMENT OF NOTES. All notes sounding simultaneously must be written so that a line drawn through the note heads will be perpendicular to the lines of the staff.

right   wrong

34. HORIZONTAL ARRANGEMENT OF NOTES.   Space between notes should be in proportion to their time values.

wrong   right

35. PLACEMENT OF CHROMATICS.   A chromatic before a note is placed on the same line or space as the note head.

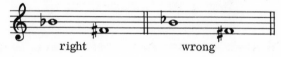

right   wrong

The effect of a chromatic lasts until the following bar-line unless it is cancelled by a natural sign, or unless the note is tied into the following measure or measures.

36. BEAMS.   Notes employing flags may be grouped together with beams.

Notes ordinarily should be beamed in terms of beat units. └────┘ indicates a beat unit.

When a group of beamed notes is placed on the staff, use a stem direction which is correct for a majority of the notes in the group.

In most vocal music, beams are used only when two or more notes are found on a single syllable.

Santa Lucia

Now 'neath   the sil - ver moon   o - cean   is   glow - ing,

The curved line connecting two or more notes of different pitch is known as a *slur*.

The Major Triad

2

THEORY AND ANALYSIS[1]

A triad is a three-note chord built in thirds, and may be constructed on any scale tone.

Scale degree	Triad number and spelling in C major[2]			
1 (tonic)	I	C	E	G
2 (supertonic)	ii	D	F	A
3 (mediant)	iii	E	G	B
4 (subdominant)	IV	F	A	C
5 (dominant)	V	G	B	D
6 (submediant)	vi	A	C	E
7 (leading tone)	vii°	B	D	F

The I triad is also known as a tonic triad, the ii triad as a supertonic triad, and so on. A triad number as used in this text and shown above indicates triad construction (review Chapter 1, section 19) as well as the location in the scale of its lowest tone.

Large numeral: major triad (I in C major = C E G)
Small numeral: minor triad (ii in C major = D F A)
Small numeral with small °: diminished triad
  (vii° in C major = B D F)
Large numeral with +: augmented triad (not found in the major scale; I+ in C major = C E G♯)

---

[1]Chapters 2 and 3 may be studied simultaneously.
[2]Triads, chords, scale passages, and other note groupings using only notes of the scale are known as *diatonic*. The seven triads listed are diatonic. These passages are *altered* when notes not in the scale are used. For example, in C major, D F♯ A is an altered triad.

15

Of these four triads, the major triad will be considered at this time. A major triad can be constructed using the first, third and fifth degrees of the major scale.

Fig. 2.1.

1   (2)   3   (4)   5

This triad conforms to the definition of a major triad, that is, counting from the lowest note, it is composed of a major third (C-E) and a minor third (E-G) in that order.

Triad Terminology

In the triad, "1" is known as the *root*; "3" of the triad is known as the *third*; "5" of the triad is known as the *fifth*. In the C major triad, C is the root, E is the 3rd, and G is the 5th.

Major Triad Spelling

Method 1. To spell a major triad, spell the intervals in the triad.

Method 2. Students lacking facility at this time in spelling intervals will find the following method convenient until such facility is developed.

There are seven basic triad spellings, using each of the seven letter names of the musical alphabet as a root. These are ACE, BDF, CEG, DFA, EGB, FAC, and GBD. Three are already major, three are minor, and one is diminished.

Group I (major)	Group II (minor)	Group III (diminished)
C E G	D F A	B D F
F A C	E G B	
G B D	A C E	
- - -	- ↑ -	- ↑ ↑

Group I. These triad spellings will be major when each letter carries the same accidental,[3] as indicated by the symbol - - -.

C E G, C♯ E♯ G♯, Cˣ Eˣ Gˣ, C♭ E♭ G♭, C♭♭ E♭♭ G♭♭
- - -   - - -   - - -   - - -   - - -

---

[3]An accidental is a chromatic sign (see Chapter 1, section 9) not found in a key signature.

Group II. These triad spellings will be major when the third carries an accidental one-half-step higher than the root and the fifth (- ↑ -).

A C♯ E,   A♯ C✗ E♯,   A♭ C E♭,   A♭♭ C♭ E♭♭
- ↑ -   - ↑ -   - ↑ -   - ↑ -

Group III. This single triad is major when the third and fifth carry an accidental one-half-step higher than the root (- ↑↑).

B D♯ F♯,   B♯ D✗ F✗,   B♭ D F,   B♭♭ D♭ F♭
- ↑ ↑   - ↑ ↑   - ↑ ↑   - ↑ ↑

Assignment 1. Major triad spelling. Use either method.

a) Spell with letter names the major triad when each of the following is the root: C, F, E, G♭, E♭, A♯, B♭, F♯, D♭, B♯

b) Spell the major triad when each of the following is the third: B, E♯, F♯, C, D, G♯, A♭, D✗, A♭♭, F✗ (Example: A—F A C)

c) Spell the major triad when each of the following is the fifth: D, C♯, E♭, B♯, A, F, F♯, D✗, E♭♭, F♭ (Example, A♭—D♭ F A♭). This assignment may be followed by or combined with Assignment 5.

Intervals in the Major Triad

The major triad contains a number of intervals which can be found by extracting and combining any two notes from the three-note triad.

1 up to 3	Major Third (M3)	3 down to 1
3 up to 5	Minor Third (m3)	5 down to 3
5 up to 1	Perfect Fourth (P4)	1 down to 5
1 up to 5	Perfect Fifth (P5)	5 down to 1
3 up to 1	Minor Sixth (m6)	1 down to 3
5 up to 3	Major Sixth (M6)	3 down to 5
1 up to 1		1 down to 1
3 up to 3	Perfect Octave (P8)	3 down to 3
5 up to 5		5 down to 5

Assignment 2. Based on a given triad, spell each of the intervals in the table of intervals. Example—D major:

M3	D up to F♯	M6	A up to F♯
m3	F♯ up to A	m6	F♯ up to D
P4	A up to D	P8	D up to D
P5	D up to A		F♯ up to F♯
			A up to A

Do the same with the following triads, or others, as assigned. G, F,

B♭, E♭, A, B, F♯, C♭, D♯, D♭. (This assignment may be followed by or combined with Assignment 6.)

Assignment 3. Spell all the intervals in the table of intervals from a given note. Example, given the note G:

M3 up	G - B	P4 down	G - D	m6 up	G - E♭	
M3 down	G - E♭	P5 up	G - D	m6 down	G - B	
m3 up	G - B♭	P5 down	G - C	P8 up	G - G	
m3 down	G - E	M6 up	G - E	P8 down	G - G	
P4 up	G - C	M6 down	G - B♭			

Do the same from any given note.

Those intervals which are found in triads, together with scale steps, are the intervals most often used in melodic writing. Figure 2.2 shows how intervals in a melodic line may imply a major triad.

Fig. 2.2

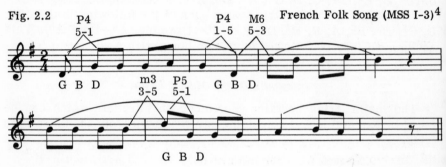

Assignment 4. Identify intervals from major triads in melodies found in Chapters 1 and 2 of *Music for Sight Singing.* In the melodies from these chapters, all skips are in the tonic triad. Copy out melodies, as assigned, and indicate intervals by number and by name as shown in Figure 2.2.

APPLICATION

WRITTEN MATERIALS

Assignment 5. Write major triads on the staff. Refer to Assignment 1. Write each triad listed in Assignment 1 in the treble and bass clefs, as shown in Figure 2.3.

---

[4]MSS refers to *Music for Sight Singing* (Englewood Cliffs, N.J.: Prentice-Hall, Inc., 1956). I-3 means Part I, melody number 3.

Fig. 2.3.

C E G   F A C   E G#B

Assignment 6. Write intervals on the staff. Refer to Assignment 2. Place each interval, ascending and descending, on the treble or bass staff as assigned, and as shown in Figure 2.4.

Fig. 2.4.

Major third   Minor third   Perfect fourth

Assignment 7. Fill in the second note of the interval according to the direction given for each interval.

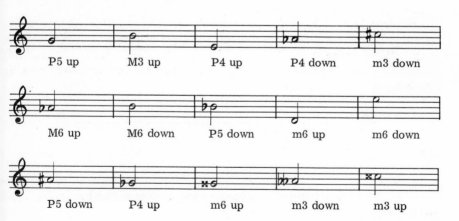

P5 up   M3 up   P4 up   P4 down   m3 down

M6 up   M6 down   P5 down   m6 up   m6 down

P5 down   P4 up   m6 up   m3 down   m3 up

EAR TRAINING AND MUSIC READING

Singing the Major Triad

Exercise 1. Singing the C major triad.

a) Sing the first five notes of the C major scale. Then, starting with 1, sing only the notes 1, 3, and 5.

Fig. 2.5.

b) Starting on 5, sing the descending scale, followed by 5, 3, and 1 only.

Fig. 2.6.

c) Sing the C major triad ascending and descending.

Fig. 2.7.

Exercise 2. a) Singing any major triad. Listen to major triads played at the piano. After each triad is sounded, sing the pattern 1-3-5-3-1.

b) Listen to the triad. Sing the root only.

Exercise 3. Singing any major triad. Play or listen to any given pitch. Call this pitch 1. Sing a major triad from this pitch.

Exercise 4. Singing any major triad from the fifth. Play or listen to any given pitch. Call this pitch 5. Sing the triad pattern 5-3-1-3-5.

Exercise 5. Singing any major triad from the third. Play or listen to any given pitch. Call this pitch 3. Sing the triad pattern 3-1-3-5-3.

Exercise 6. Repeat Exercises 2, 3, 4, and 5. Instead of singing the numbers 1-3-5-3-1, sing with chord spellings when the name of the first pitch is given.

Identifying the Soprano Note in the Triad

A characteristic feature of the music of the period 1650-1900 is the use of a succession of chords, the upper voice of which is a melodic line. Any familiar hymn will provide an example of this procedure. Listen to the melody line of Figure 2.8, then sing it back with the piano. Note in singing that there are places where the melody pauses. These pauses are somewhat analagous to punctuation marks in language reading; they mark the point at which an idea seems to end, after which a new idea starts afresh. In music, these points are known as *cadences*. In the hymn, Figure 2.8[5], four cadence points are discernible (measures 4, 8, 12, and 16). The first three cadences do not seem as final as the fourth cadence—although they are preliminary stopping points, the fourth cadence is the only final stopping point.

Sing the same hymn melody with the piano accompaniment in chords. When chords are used, there is no change in the location of the cadence points. The succession of chords (usually two) at a cadence point is known as a *harmonic cadence.*

---

[5]This hymn was written by the American composer Lowell Mason in 1824. Although a Protestant hymn, it is believed to have been inspired by a chant from the Roman Catholic liturgy. There are several chants from which the hymn could be derived; one is shown in Figures 2.9 and 2.10 in both plainsong notation and modern notation. This plainsong can be found on page 148 of the *Liber Usualis* (Tournay, 1938), a collection of the most used music of the Roman Catholic liturgy.

Fig. 2.8.

Fig. 2.9.

Fig. 2.10.

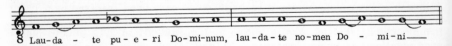

Lau-da - te pu-e-ri Do-mi-num, lau-da-te no-men Do - mi-ni——

The following exercises are designed as an aid in identifying the function of the soprano note, based upon the recognition of melodic and harmonic cadence points.

Exercise 7. Identify the final soprano (melody) note in the cadence.

    a) Listen to a phrase of music, with harmony.

    b) Sing the melody line with piano.

    c) Listen to the final chord of the phrase; sing melody note.

    d) Sing the chord pattern (1-3-5) and identify the soprano note as 1, 3, or 5.

Exercise 8. Same as Exercise 7, but sing back melody line without piano, after having heard it played at the piano.

Exercise 9. Identify soprano notes of the harmonic cadence.

    a) Listen to a phrase of music; sing back last two notes.

    b) Listen to each chord of the cadence separately. Identify the soprano note of each as in Exercise 7d.

Exercise 10. Same as Exercise 9, but listen to two-chord cadence progressions only.

Exercise 11. Identify the soprano note of a single triad. Listen to a single triad and identify soprano note as before.

Exercise 12. Spelling the major triad. The name of the soprano note will be given. Identify the soprano note by number, then spell the chord. Example: F♯ is given as the soprano note. Listen to the chord played.

Fig. 2.11.

Identify the soprano as the third of the triad. If F♯ is the third, then the triad is spelled D F♯ A.

Upon completion of Exercise 19 (playing the triad at the keyboard) in this chapter, students working in pairs can practice Exercises 11 and 12 outside the classroom. One student of the pair will play a triad and announce the name of the soprano note while the other proceeds with either Exercise 11 or 12. After approximately ten chords, the students should change places. Both students will derive much valuable practice in both keyboard harmony and ear training.

Intervals

Exercise 13. Singing intervals from the triad by number.

a) Sing a major triad from a given pitch, using the numbers 1-3-5-3-1. Then sing two-note combinations (intervals) from this triad, as directed.

Fig. 2.12.

1 3 5 3 1   1 3   3 5   1 5   3 1   etc.

b) Sing the triad with additional upper or lower tones within the singing range. Sing interval combinations as directed.

Fig. 2.13.

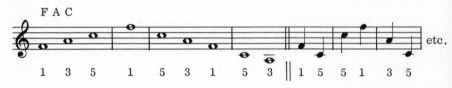

F A C

1 3 5   1 5 3   1 5 3   1 5   5 1   3 5   etc.

Exercise 14. Sing a given interval from a given pitch, using triad numbers. Sing aloud, or mentally, the basic triad before singing the interval. For example, if G is given, call G 3 and sing 3 up to 5.

Fig. 2.14.

3   (1   3   5)   3   5

Exercise 15. Identify melodic or harmonic intervals aurally. (An interval composed of two notes sounded simultaneously is known as a *harmonic interval;* when composed of two notes sounded in succession it is known as a *melodic interval*.)

a) (1) You will hear a triad at the piano, followed by an interval (melodic or harmonic) from that triad. Sing the interval on la.

(2) Sing complete triad using 1-3-5-3-1.

(3) Sing interval again, using correct numbers.

Fig. 2.15.

b) Same as *a)* above, but instead of singing the interval with numbers, write the correct number relationship, for example " 1 up to 5" in Figure 2.15.

c) Same as above except that triad will not be played.

d) With continued practice, sing or write interval with correct numbers immediately after hearing interval.

Exercise 16. Identify intervals by name when played at the piano. Listen to the interval; identify the interval numbers and give the name of the interval.

Exercise 17. Sing interval when name of interval is given and one note of interval is given at the piano.

Exercise 18. Write intervals on the staff from dictation. The first note of the interval will be given; place this on the staff. Listen to the interval, then write:

a) the numbers of the interval
b) the name of the interval
c) the triad spelling
d) the second note of the interval

Fig. 2.16.

After sufficient practice, continue drill by omitting steps *a)* and *c)*.

Upon completion of Exercise 20 (playing intervals at the keyboard), students working in pairs can aid each other in mastering Exercises 16-18. One student will play the interval while the other student identifies the interval.

KEYBOARD HARMONY

Exercise 19. Playing the major triad with the root in the bass at the keyboard.

a) Spell the triad.

b) Find the root of the triad in the left hand. Do not play.

c) Place the little finger of the right hand on the given soprano note. Do not play.

d) Find the other two notes of the triad immediately below the soprano note, using the right hand. Do not play.

e) Play all four notes of the triad simultaneously. Sample problem: Play the D major triad with the third in the soprano.

Fig. 2.17.

The triad is commonly played and written in four parts, as above. In adding the extra note, one of the members of the triad is *doubled*, that is, there will be two of that member. The root of the triad is usually doubled.

Exercise 20. At the keyboard, play any given interval based on a given triad.

Procedure	*Example*
a) Listen to directions	*a)* Play 5 up to 1 in the A♭ major triad.
b) Spell the triad	*b)* A♭ C E♭.
c) Spell interval	*c)* 5 up to 1 is E♭ up to A♭
d) Play interval	*d)*

Rhythm (I)

THEORY AND ANALYSIS

Since music exists in time, a given pitch must sound for a certain length of time until it is replaced by another pitch, which may sound for the same or a different length of time. These durations need to be measured before they can be set down on paper to become part of the music score.

The Beat

The standard of measurement in musical time is the *beat*. The beat is not a fixed length of time; it can be long or short according to the character of the particular musical composition. The nature of the beat is commonly experienced by most persons when listening to music. For example, when walking to the accompaniment of a military march, your footsteps mark off equal measurements of time which can be considered as beats. The slower the music, the longer the beat, and conversely, the faster the music, the shorter the beat. The metronome set at 80 establishes a beat of moderate speed; beat durations range from a beat of long duration (approximately M.M. 50) to a beat of short duration (approximately M.M. 140). The tempo of a composition is directly related to the length of the beat—music in a slow tempo is comprised of beats of long duration, music in a fast tempo of beats of short duration.

Exercise 21. Listening for beats. Listen to music played by the instructor. With the right hand, make taps of equal time durations. Be sure not to tap the unequal durations you may hear in the melody or other prominent part; your taps should be of equal duration and conform comfortably to the tempo of the music.

It will be noted that beats tend to group themselves, one beat assuming more importance than following beats. The more important, or stronger, beat recurs regularly, usually marking off groups of 2, 3, or 4 beats.

Fig. 3.1.

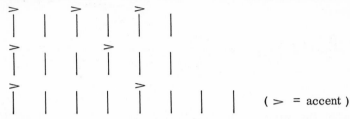

(> = accent)

Exercise 22. Listening for beat groupings. Listen to music, as in Exercise 21. When the strong beat is located, count aloud 1-2 or 1-2-3 as the case may be. (In listening, it is difficult to distinguish between the two-beat and four-beat groupings.)

Two varieties of the beat exist. These can best be illustrated by listening to two different folk songs, Figures 3.2 and 3.4 In each folk song, the beats are in groups of two, but the nature of the beat differs in each of the two songs.

Fig. 3.2.   Spanish Folk Song (MSS I-9)

Listen to the melody in Figure 3.2. Note that each beat in this melody can be divided into two parts. This can be demonstrated by tapping the beats in the right hand, and with the left hand making two taps for each beat in the right hand.

Fig. 3.3.

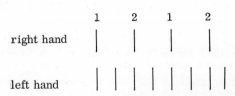

Fig. 3.4.   German Folk Song (MSS I-164)

Listen to the melody in Figure 3.4. Note that each beat in this melody can be divided into three parts. This can be demonstrated by tapping the beats in the right hand, and, with the left hand, making three taps for each beat in the right hand.

Fig. 3.5.

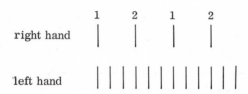

The above procedure is known as dividing the beat. A beat which can be divided into two parts is known as a *simple* beat, a division often called "background of two." A beat which can be divided into three parts is known as a *compound* beat, and is often called "background of three."

Exercise 23. Listen to music examples: *a)* determine whether the background of the beat is simple or compound and, *b)* as in Exercise 22, determine whether the beats are in groupings of 2 or 3.

Meter

The meter of a piece of music is the basic scheme of beat groupings used; most music has a meter of two, three, or four beats per measure. Meter is not to be confused with rhythm. The term "rhythm" indicates the pattern of longer and shorter note values used; the sum total of the note or rest values in each measure will be equal to the number of beats per measure.

Fig. 3.6.   Hungarian Folk Song (MSS I-13)

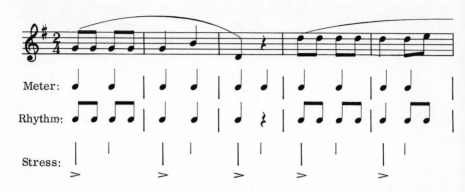

The Time Signature

It is the function of the time signature (meter signature) to indicate the meter of the piece (how many beats per measure) and the kind of notation to be used (what kind of a note gets one beat).

Simple Time. Music in which the beat is a simple beat is said to be in simple time. Since a simple beat is divisible into two parts, any note value divisible into two parts may be used to represent a beat. Therefore, any undotted note may be used to represent a beat.

Each time signature in Table 1 is derived by multiplying the number of beats per measure by the value of the note (indicated here as a fraction) assigned to receive one beat.

TABLE 1

SIMPLE TIME SIGNATURES

Beat note	2 beats per measure (Duple)	3 beats per measure (Triple)	4 beats per measure (Quadruple)
$\circ$ ($\frac{1}{1}$)	$\frac{2}{1}$	$\frac{3}{1}$	$\frac{4}{1}$
$\textrm{d}$ ($\frac{1}{2}$)	$\frac{2}{2}$ or $\textrm{C}\!\!\mid$	$\frac{3}{2}$	$\frac{4}{2}$
$\textrm{J}$ ($\frac{1}{4}$)	$\frac{2}{4}$	$\frac{3}{4}$	$\frac{4}{4}$ or C
$\textrm{♪}$ ($\frac{1}{8}$)	$\frac{2}{8}$	$\frac{3}{8}$	$\frac{4}{8}$
$\textrm{♪}$ ($\frac{1}{16}$)	$\frac{2}{16}$	$\frac{3}{16}$	$\frac{4}{16}$
$\textrm{♪}$ ($\frac{1}{32}$)	$\frac{2}{32}$	$\frac{3}{32}$	$\frac{4}{32}$

Theoretically, this table could be extended indefinitely. Signatures with denominators of 4, 2, 8 and 16 are those most used, and in that order of frequency.

Observe from Table 1 that in simple time, the numerators of time signatures are 2, 3 and 4.

2 = duple simple time (meter)
3 = triple simple time
4 = quadruple simple time

Therefore, the time signature $\frac{2}{4}$ is to be interpreted as follows: $\frac{2}{4}$ indicates that the music is in duple simple time, meaning that there are two beats in the measure, each beat divisible into two parts; the quarter note is used to represent the beat, and it is divisible into two eighth notes.

Fig. 3.7.

Exercise 24. Explain verbally, or by diagram as in Figure 3.7, the meaning of the following time signatures.

$$\frac{3}{4}, \ \frac{4}{4}, \ \frac{2}{8}, \ \frac{3}{2}, \ \frac{3}{8}, \ \frac{4}{16}, \ \frac{4}{2}$$

Compound Time.   Music in which the beat is a compound beat is said to be in compound time. Since a compound beat is divisible into three parts, any note value divisible into three parts may be used to represent a beat.   Therefore, any dotted note may be used to represent a beat. Table 2, like the one for simple time, could theoretically be extended indefinitely.   Most commonly used are those with denominators of 8, 4 and 16, in that order of frequency of usage.

Observe from Table 2 that in compound time the numerators of the time signatures are 6, 9 and 12.

‣ 6 = duple compound time
9 = triple compound time
12 = quadruple compound time

Therefore, the time signature $\frac{6}{8}$ is interpreted as follows: $\frac{6}{8}$ indicates that the music is in duple compound time, meaning that there are two beats in the measure, each beat being divisible into three

TABLE 2

COMPOUND TIME SIGNATURES

Beat note	2 beats per measure (Duple)	3 beats per measure (Triple)	4 beats per measure (Quadruple)
$\circ \cdot (\frac{3}{2})$	$\frac{6}{2}$	$\frac{9}{2}$	$\frac{12}{2}$
$\downarrow \cdot (\frac{3}{4})$	$\frac{6}{4}$	$\frac{9}{4}$	$\frac{12}{4}$
$\downarrow \cdot (\frac{3}{8})$	$\frac{6}{8}$	$\frac{9}{8}$	$\frac{12}{8}$
$\downarrow \cdot (\frac{3}{16})$	$\frac{6}{16}$	$\frac{9}{16}$	$\frac{12}{16}$
$\downarrow \cdot (\frac{3}{32})$	$\frac{6}{32}$	$\frac{9}{32}$	$\frac{12}{32}$

parts; the dotted quarter is used to represent the beat, and it is divisible into three eighth notes.

Fig. 3.8.

Note that the compound time signatures do not indicate the number of beats per measure and the note value receiving one beat as conveniently as do the simple time signatures. Actually, the upper number of the compound signature indicates the number of *divided beats* per measure, while the lower number states the kind of note used to indicate a divided beat.

Occasionally contemporary composers will write a compound signature with the actual number of beats in the numerator and a note value in the denominator: $\frac{2}{\downarrow \cdot}$ instead of $\frac{6}{8}$; $\frac{3}{\downarrow}$ instead of $\frac{9}{16}$ and so on.

Fig. 3.9.   Paul Hindemith, String Trio, op. 34

Sehr lebhaft

(instead of $\frac{6}{4}$)

Exercise 25. Explain verbally, or by diagram as in Figure 3.8, the meaning of the following time signatures.

$$\frac{6}{4}, \; \frac{9}{8}, \; \frac{12}{8}, \; \frac{6}{16}, \; \frac{12}{4}, \; \frac{9}{2}$$

Exceptions

In any time signature, the upper number always indicates how many of the note values expressed by the lower number will be found in any one measure. Usually, the time signature expresses rhythmic concepts just as presented, but exceptions do exist.

a) Numerator of 4. In a fast tempo, there may be actually two beats per measure. In a fast $\frac{4}{4}$, the beat may be a half note, two half notes per measure. Sometimes this is indicated in the music by the term "alla breve" or by the signature ₵. (See *Music for Sight Singing,* Part I, Numbers 30 and 31.)

b) Numerator of 3. In a fast tempo, there may be actually one beat per measure. In a fast $\frac{3}{4}$, the beat may be a ♩. , divisible into three quarter notes. Thus the effect is that of compound time, one beat per measure. The *scherzo* movements from the various Beethoven symphonies illustrate this effect. (See also *Music for Sight Singing,* Part I, Number 66.)

c) Numerator of 2, 3 or 4. In a slow tempo, the division of the note value indicated in the denominator may become the beat note. In a slow $\frac{2}{4}$, the eighth note may become the beat, with four beats per measure. (See Beethoven, Sonata for Piano No. 3, Op. 2, No. 3, second movement; also *Music for Sight Singing,* Chapter 21.)

d) Numerator of 6, 9, 12. In a slow tempo, the numerator may indicate the number of beats per measure. These beats are rarely equal in stress. Usually the first note and every third note thereafter receives a stress; this preserves the impression of compound time.

Fig. 3.10.

(See Beethoven, Sonata for Piano No. 7, Op. 10, No. 3, second movement; also *Music for Sight Singing,* Chapter 21.)

Terminology variant. A simple time signature is sometimes defined as one with a numerator of 2 or 3; a compound time signature is one whose numerator is a compound of 2 or 3. Thus $\frac{4}{4}$ is a compound of $\frac{2}{4}$ ($\frac{4}{4} = \frac{2}{4} \times 2$), $\frac{6}{8} = \frac{3}{8} \times 2$, $\frac{9}{4} = \frac{3}{4} \times 3$, and so on.

APPLICATION

WRITTEN MATERIALS

Assignment 8. Place a correct time signature before each musical example. The first measure of an example may be incomplete, in which case the last measure is also incomplete; the two partial measures equal one complete measure in time value. In a few cases, more than one correct signature is possible.

Assignment 9. Find examples of time signatures in music scores, particularly those other than the commonly used $\frac{2}{4}$, $\frac{3}{4}$, $\frac{4}{4}$ and $\frac{6}{8}$. Copy out one or two measures of the music, including the time signature; indicate source of music including composer, title, publisher and page number.

Rhythmic Transcription

Music written with a given time signature may be rewritten following any other time signature with the same numerator.

Fig. 3.11.

a)

b)

Performance of examples in each pair would be identical, assuming both have the same tempo indication.

Assignment 10. From Part I of *Music for Sight Singing,* write each melody with the time signature indicated.

a) No. 1 in $\frac{4}{2}$, $\frac{4}{8}$ e) No. 38 in $\frac{6}{4}$, $\frac{6}{16}$

b) No. 18 in $\frac{4}{4}$ f) No. 44 in $\frac{6}{8}$, $\frac{6}{4}$

c) No. 25 in $\frac{3}{8}$, $\frac{3}{16}$ g) No. 109 in $\frac{12}{4}$, $\frac{12}{16}$

d) No. 31 in $\frac{4}{4}$, $\frac{4}{2}$ h) No. 170 in $\frac{9}{4}$, $\frac{9}{16}$

EAR TRAINING AND MUSIC READING

The ability to read rhythm demonstrates comprehension of the meaning of the printed rhythmic symbols. This ability is one of the two required for successful sight singing, the other being comprehension of the printed pitch symbols.

Use of the conductor's beats of 2, 3 and 4 will facilitate the development of rhythmic reading ability. Each of these conductor's beats is characterized by a preparatory up-beat, followed by a down-beat on the first beat of the measure. The up-beat is the preparation for the following down-beat; the down-beat drops in a straight line and describes a small bounce at the instant the first beat occurs. After the down-beat, each of the conductor's beats follows a different course.

Fig. 3.12.

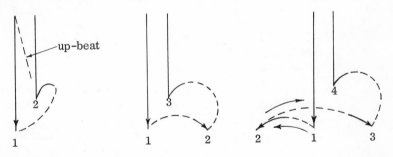

At the completion of one measure, the last beat of the measure is the up-beat of the next measure.

Exercise 26. Practice each of the conductor's beats before a mirror and with a metronome. Set the metronome at a slow rate at first (about M.M. 50). These movements must become completely automatic, so that when you read rhythm or sing at sight, your attention can be devoted to the musical notation.

Exercise 27. Add simple background to each of these conductor's beats by tapping twice with the left hand to each beat of the right hand. In doing so, you are conducting duple simple, triple simple, and quadruple simple times. Follow all directions given in Exercise 26.

Exercise 28. Practice the conductor's beats (2, 3 and 4) adding a compound background by tapping three times with the left hand to each beat in the right hand. In doing so, you are conducting duple compound, triple compound, and quadruple compound times. Follow other directions given in Exercise 26.

Rhythmic Reading

Reading should be done with rhythmic syllables. For notes which fall on the beat use the number of the beat in the measure. When the note is held for more than one beat, hold the number of the beat on which the note started.

Fig. 3.13.   German Folk Song (MSS I-1)

Simple Time. When the beat is divided into two equal parts, the second half of the beat may receive the syllable ta (tah).[1]

Fig. 3.14.   Spanish Folk Song (MSS I-25)

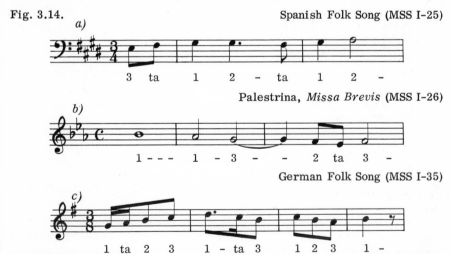

Palestrina, *Missa Brevis* (MSS I-26)

German Folk Song (MSS I-35)

---

[1]Syllables other than ta may be used to read durations shorter than the beat, if desired. Rhythmic reading is more precise, and therefore more likely to be accurate, if the rhythmic syllable begins with an explosive consonant.

Compound Time. When the beat is divided into three parts, the second and third division of each beat may receive the syllable ta.

Fig. 3.15.   German Folk Song (MSS I-40)

ta   1   ta   2 ta ta   1   2   ta   1   ta 2 ta ta   1

American Folk Song (Indiana) (MSS I-51)

ta   1   ta   2   ta   ta   1   ta   ta   2   ta

Before reading, make the following preparations:

a) Review the meaning of the time signature.

b) Choose the appropriate conductor's beat.

c) Start the conductor's beat and background at least one measure before beginning to read.

Try to read each piece of music through without stopping. If you make an error, do not stop to correct it, but keep going. The conductor's downbeat always coincides with a bar line in the music, and it will help you keep your place. At the end of the piece, go back to review the reasons for any errors you made and reread those places to correct the errors.

Exercise 29.[2] Rhythmic reading in simple time. Ample material may be found in *Music for Sight Singing,* using all melodies in Chapters 1, 3 and 6, and all other melodies in Part I which are in simple time. These melodies in simple time use the beat and its division into two parts only.

Exercise 30. Rhythmic reading in compound time. Material may be found in *Music for Sight Singing,* using all melodies in Chapters 2, 4, and 7, and all other melodies in Part I which are in compound time. These melodies in compound time use the beat and its division into three parts only.

Rhythmic Dictation

This is the converse of rhythmic reading. In rhythmic reading the rhythmic symbols are converted into sound. In rhythmic dictation, the rhythmic sounds are converted into notation. At this point,

---

[2]Upon completion of Exercise 29, you may begin work in Chapter 4.

rhythmic dictation will contain the same problems as studied in rhythmic reading.

Exercise 31. Rhythmic dictation, simple time.

Follow this procedure in taking rhythmic dictation.

a) The time signature will be announced. Write this on your paper.

b) At the given signal, make the proper conductor's beat and tap the background.

c) Listen to the melody played, while conducting.

d) Sing back the melody, aloud or silently as directed, still using the conductor's beat.

e) Write rhythmic notation on your paper.

Had melody Number 1 from *Music for Sight Singing* been dictated, your solution would be as follows:

Exercise 32. Rhythmic dictation, compound time.   Follow directions listed in Exercise 31.

Self-Help Procedures

In listening to a melody being dictated, it is of utmost importance that the student *memorize* the melody as soon as possible, since it is impossible to write on paper that which cannot be recalled to mind. The ability to remember the sounds heard will be equally important in later studies, such as melodic and harmonic dictation.

Students working in pairs can be of great assistance to each other in training melodic memory or rhythmic dictation outside regular classroom time.   These procedures may be followed.

Memory. Using *Music for Sight Singing,* Student A chooses a melody. From this melody he plays one to four measures. Student B immediately sings the phrase back.   If there is an error or if it is incomplete, the procedure is repeated until a correct response is achieved.   Continued practice will reduce the number of hearings necessary to achieve a correct response. When the number of playings is reduced to one, extend the length of the melody.

Dictation. Using *Music for Sight Singing,* Student A chooses a melody and announces the time signature.   Student B makes the appropriate conductor's beat, with background.   Student A plays one phrase which Student B sings back, using rhythmic syllables. Repeat playing and singing until phrase is sung back correctly.   Then write the rhythmic notation only on paper. Aim to reduce the number of hearings necessary and to extend the amount of material heard at one time.

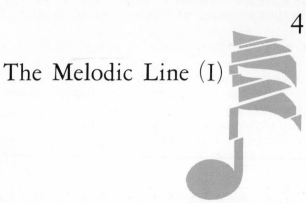

The Melodic Line (I)

THEORY AND ANALYSIS[1]

A melodic line consists of a succession of tones. Pitch-wise this succession usually consists of scale steps, together with intervals of a larger size. Rhythm-wise it consists of notes displaying varying degrees of duration. Melodies may be simple or difficult, depending on the simplicity or complexity of their pitch and rhythmic elements. In many melodies these elements are contained within a formal structure.

Pitch. A melody in simplest form may consist of scale steps only, (see Fig. 2.8) but such melodies are comparatively uncommon. More usual is a melody incorporating both scale-wise intervals and larger intervals. Having studied the intervals in the major triad, we will begin the study of the melodic line using those melodies which use intervals in a single triad—the tonic triad—as well as scale-wise intervals.

Rhythm. The simplest kind of rhythmic pattern in a melody would be the use of a single note value. Such melodies are uncommon. Melodic interest is heightened by contrast in the durations of pitches. This contrast can be very simple, as demonstrated by melody Number 14 from _Music for Sight Singing,_ which consists of eighth notes only except for a single quarter note at the beginning of measures four and eight. Melodies 1 and 10 are only slightly more complex. In rhythmic reading, observe how few rhythmic patterns

---

[1]The study of each of these skills in simple time may begin upon completion of rhythmic reading and dictation in simple time from Chapter 3. It is suggested that the study of sight singing and melodic dictation precede that of melodic composition.

are used in any one melody and how often rhythmic patterns are repeated.

Form. Most music is written in some orderly arrangement. In
the music of western civilization, certain patterns or plans of musical construction have come to be commonly (though not exclusively)
used. These patterns are known as musical _forms_.

A melody may consist of a group of _phrases_. A phrase in music
is a group or stream of notes, the last of which seems to mark a
natural resting place, either temporary or final. This phenomenon
has already been described earlier as a cadence (page 21). The
usual length of a phrase is four measures, as illustrated by Figures
4.1 and 4.2.

Fig. 4.1.   German Folk Song (MSS I-28)

In this melody, the first phrase ends with a cadence on the tonic
note, and the whole phrase is marked off with a phrase-mark extending from the first note to the last note of the phrase. A phrase
may also consist of two or more distinct units, called _motives_. The
phrase in Figure 4.2 is composed of two two-measure motives; the

Fig. 4.2.   German Folk Song (MSS I-1)

motives combine to make a phrase. The motive can be identified by
the fact that it is a unit of melody smaller than a phrase, usually
identifiable by a pause in the melodic line or in the rhythm. Note
that the phrase-mark is used to indicate the length of the motive.

Two phrases may combine to form a _period_. In a period, the first
phrase, called the _antecedent phrase_, usually ends on a temporary (HALF)
cadence (lacking a feeling of complete finality). This is accomplished
by ending the phrase on a note of the V triad (Figure 4.3) or, less
often, on a note of the tonic triad (Figure 4.4). The second phrase,
called the _consequent phrase_, then ends on a final cadence. This
last note is usually the tonic note, or at least some note of the tonic
triad.

Periods may be *parallel* or *contrasting*. A period is parallel when the two phrases are similar in some respect. Usually the beginnings of each phrase are identical, as in Figure 4.3, but any marked melodic similarity in the two phrases, such as the similar melodic contour in Figure 4.4, will justify analysis as a parallel period. When the two phrases of a period lack any specific or general similarity, the period is contrasting, as in Figure 4.5.

Fig. 4.3. Parallel Period   American Folk Song (Tennessee) (MSS I-43)

Fig. 4.4. Parallel Period   Mexican Folk Song (MSS I-14)

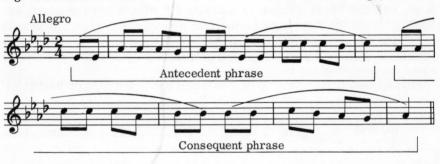

Fig. 4.5. Contrasting Period   Italian Folk Song (MSS I-38)

Phrases are also classified according to the rhythmic placement of their first and last notes. Phrases beginning on a strong beat are said to have a *masculine beginning,* phrases beginning on a weak beat a *feminine beginning.* Similarly, phrases ending on a strong beat have a *masculine ending* and phrases ending on a weak beat a *feminine ending.* The four possible combinations of masculine and feminine beginnings and endings can be found in Chapter 1 of *Music for Sight Singing.*

Fig. 4.6.

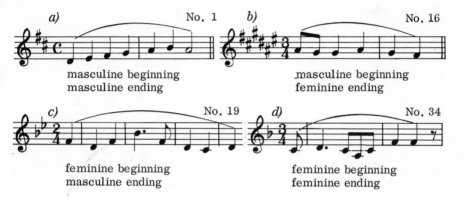

Parts *a)*, *b)* and *d)* of Figure 4.6 are motives. The principle is the same for entire phrases.

Usually each phrase of a period uses the same type of beginning and ending, though exceptions may be noted. (See *Music for Sight Singing,* melody Number I-106.)

There are many exceptions to these statements concerning musical form. A careful study of the melodies used for sight singing will reveal many variations of musical forms, including phrases of lengths other than four measures, cadences on tones other than those previously indicated, and combinations of repetitions of either phrase or parts of phrases. But for the first attempts in melodic analysis and melody writing, the student should be satisfied to confine his efforts to the four-measure phrase and to the parallel or contrasting eight-measure period.

Assignment 11. From Chapters 1-2 of *Music for Sight Singing,* analyze any of the following melodies: 1, 2, 31, 32, 34, 44, 48, 49, 51. These are all regular periods. Copy out each melody; indicate *a)* phrase lengths, *b)* whether parallel or contrasting period, *c)* location of cadence points, and *d)* nature of the beginning and ending of each phrase. Use this example as a guide.

Fig. 4.7.   Spanish Folk Song (MSS I-9)

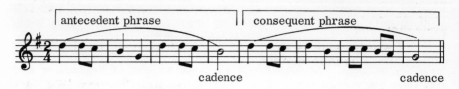

Each phrase has a masculine beginning and a masculine ending. The two phrases make a contrasting period.

APPLICATION

WRITTEN MATERIALS

Melodic Composition

The simplicity of *writing* a good melody can be observed through careful study of the melodies in Chapters 1-2 of *Music for Sight Singing*. These demonstrate how effectively a limited amount of technical material can produce a pleasing musical composition. These materials already studied are

   a) The scale.

   b) Intervals in the tonic triad.

   c) Rhythm—no note value smaller than the beat note and its division into two parts (in simple time) and into three parts (compound time).

Before writing a melody, special characteristics of the melodic line must be investigated.

   a) Scale-wise progressions are always good, but avoid more than five or six scale tones in the same direction. Melody Number 1, starting with six scale tones ascending, demonstrates the usual limit of successive scale tones in one direction.

   b) Skips (intervals of a third or larger) are usually limited to not more than two in the same direction, after which the melodic line progresses in the opposite direction.

Fig. 4.8.   English Folk Song (MSS I-6)

Exceptions can be found in melodies 11 and 19, in which the melody continues scale-wise in the same direction after two leaps in the same direction.

After a large skip (a fifth or larger) it is almost always best to change direction immediately.

Fig. 4.9.   Mexican Folk Song (MSS I-14)

c) *Repetition* from one phrase to another has already been shown under form (melody Number 1). Repetition of smaller units of the melody are also effective.

Fig. 4.10.   Spanish Folk Song (MSS I-9)

A *sequence* is similar to repetition except that the repeated material appears at a new pitch level. In the following example, measures 3 and 4 each are a sequence of measure 2. (See also melodies 10, 24 and 28.)

Fig. 4.11.   German Folk Song (MSS I-20)

Sequence need not be exact, but may be modified to some extent. The last two measures below are a sequence of the previous two measures, though differing by one note.

Fig. 4.12.   Spanish Folk Song (MSS I-25)

d) The highest note of a melody (the *climax* note) is usually not repeated during the course of the phrase, and often not repeated during the course of a period. Because it is the highest note, it tends to stand out from the rest of the piece and repetition diminishes its effectiveness. The same rule applies to the lowest note of a melody (*anti-climax* note), though not as strictly.

e) The leading tone (seventh scale step) must be treated carefully. As its name implies, it *leads* to the tonic. In an *ascending* scale passage, the leading tone must progress to the tonic. In a *descending* passage, the leading tone may progress either way. Observe these characteristics of the leading tone in melodies 29 and 35 from Part I of *Music for Sight Singing*. A descending passage should not begin with a leading tone.

Assignment 12. Write original four-measure melodies demonstrating each of the four possible phrase classifications (masculine and feminine beginnings and endings).

Review the following before writing, and check the melody you have written against these points.

a) Use only scale-wise passages and skips in the tonic triad.

b) Use a simple meter; use no note value smaller than the beat note and its division into two parts. Avoid complex rhythm patterns.

c) Use scale-wise patterns, skips, repetitions and sequences as discussed in this chapter.

d) Be sure each phrase ends with a cadential feeling: on a note of the V triad (temporary) or a note of the I triad (final).

Assignment 13. *a)* Use melodies from assignment 12, each as one phrase of a period. Write a second phrase to complete the period.

b) Write completely original periods.

Assignment 14. Continue work with assignments 12-13 writing in compound time.

The test of a good melody is its singability. Playing the melody on the piano will not necessarily reveal a defect, since almost any melody can easily be played. If, in singing, there is an awkward interval or section, try to determine the cause of the defect and rewrite as much as necessary to make the melody easily singable.

EAR TRAINING AND MUSIC READING

Sight Singing

One of the skills demanded of the professional musician is the ability to "hear" a musical score merely by looking at it. This is essential, for instance, to any musician who expects to direct a musical ensemble, whether it be band, orchestra or choir. The director of such an ensemble must look at his score and know what sounds to expect from his organization. He has to recognize whether the sounds played or sung are the same as those written in his score, and what specific errors are being made by the performers. If the director cannot do this, he is merely a "stick-waver" and unable to offer his musicians any competent assistance in the reproduction of the musical score.

This all-important ability can be developed in several ways: *a)* through ear-training exercises, already begun in Chapter 2, *b)* through exercises in dictation, begun in Chapter 2, and *c)* through sight singing. In sight singing, the student is asked to look at a piece of music he has never seen before and then sing that music without recourse to any instrument. When this can be done correctly, it demonstrates the student's ability to comprehend mentally the symbols on the printed page. Reading music on an instrument does not prove this skill conclusively; a pianist, for example, may interpret a note on the staff as a fingering and play the note correctly without knowing beforehand what it will sound like.

Sight singing involves the simultaneous use of two reading skills —the reading of rhythm and the reading of pitch. The former skill has been studied in Chapter 3; at this point the study of the skill of reading pitches will be added to that of reading rhythm. Initial sight singing experience may be gained from *Music for Sight Singing,* Chapters 1-2, using those melodies in major keys. These contain only scale-wise intervals and intervals in the tonic triad. Follow carefully the directions given on pages 3-4 of *Music for Sight Singing.*

Melodic Dictation

In melodic dictation, the student is asked to write on the staff a melody he hears performed. This is a skill closely related to sight singing; while in sight singing, the student interprets notation as pitch, in melodic dictation the student interprets pitch as notation. Melodic dictation is also a continuation of the skills learned in rhythmic dictation, with the added ability to write the correct pitch. As in sight singing, at this point all dictated melodies will be diatonic and scale-wise, with occasional intervals in the tonic triad, and with rhythm no more difficult than that of previous rhythm dictation exercises.

Exercise 33. Melodic dictation, simple time. Follow this procedure.

a) The name of the key will be given. Write the key signature on the staff (or the name of the first note will be given; write this on the staff and determine the key signature after *c)* below).

b) The time signature will be given. Write this on the staff.

c) Making the conductor's beat and tapping the background, listen to the melody played by the instructor.

d) On the second playing, sing the melody with the piano.

e) Sing the melody without piano, still conducting and tapping.

f) Write the melody on the staff. If it seems particularly difficult, write out the rhythm first above the staff.

e) Listen to a final playing to check your work.

After sufficient practice, eliminate steps *d)* and *e)*.

Exercise 34. Melodic dictation, compound time. Follow directions given in Exercise 33.

Success in melodic dictation, as in rhythmic dictation, depends upon the ability to memorize the melody heard. Review the comments and directions for the development of musical memory found on page 39.

KEYBOARD HARMONY

Exercise 35. Play melodies from Chapters 1-2 of *Music for Sight Singing,* melodies written for Assignments 12-14, or other melodies as assigned, at the keyboard. Before playing the melody, play the tonic triad of the key. While playing, observe the melodic skips and mentally relate each to the tonic triad.

5

The Connection of Chords

THEORY AND ANALYSIS

Elementary Principles of Part-Writing

Part-writing is a process used to connect a series of chords in a musical composition. Such a series of chords can be seen by re-examining the hymn in Fig. 2.8. Each chord of the first phrase can be extracted in order and spelled as follows:

FAC   FAC   CEG   FAC   GB♭D   F♯AC   GB♭D   FAC   CEG   FAC

This set of triads is not strung together haphazardly to form the hymn. We must investigate the principles of chord connection in order to know in what voice (soprano, alto, and so on) any note of a chord will occur. Why, for example, is the alto note in the fourth chord an F? Why not C? or A?

From your work in sight singing, melodic dictation and melodic composition, you have learned that the primary qualification of a good melody is its singability. Most music is written in more than one part. Although it can be analyzed as a series of chords, as was done above, we can also consider the soprano, alto, tenor and bass parts as separate melodies. Each part must be melodic to insure that it will be easily performable and the ensemble will sound well together. Taking this first phrase of the hymn, we could use the same tune and chord spellings, but arrange the notes of the lower voices in haphazard order, as shown below. Note that the chord progression (the harmony) is identical to that in Fig. 2.8; only the arrangement of notes within each chord is different.

Fig. 5.1.

FAC　FAC　CEG　FAC　GB♭D F♯AC　GB♭D　FAC　CEG　FAC

As this "arrangement" is played at the piano, try to sing the alto part. It is difficult because the alto line is poor melodically. Now compare the alto line above with the alto line of the same phrase in Fig. 2.8. Which is easier to sing?

Fig. 5.2.

The same comparison may be made between the two tenor lines.

The rules of part-writing,[1] the first of which appear in this chapter, are designed to make it possible to connect chords in such a way that each horizontal (melodic) part is as smooth and performable as possible. Knowledge of part-writing techniques will aid you in arranging and composing music; it will also give you a standard by which to judge the performability of music when selecting it for yourself or for the group under your direction.

For the first part-writing project, the single triad will be placed on the staff. The triad will be written in four voices—soprano, alto, tenor and bass, conforming to the four ranges of the human voice. When the treble and bass staves are used, the soprano and alto voices appear on the treble staff, and the tenor and bass voices appear on the bass staff.

---

[1] A complete list of the rules of part-writing can be found in Appendix I. It should be understood that these rules exist only for pedagogical convenience. They are not inviolable; rather, each rule expresses the procedure that composers of the past have used most often in a given musical situation. Exceptions abound and will be discussed in the text at appropriate times.

In part-writing the single triad, four factors must be taken into consideration, *a)* voice range, *b)* doubling, *c)* triad position and *d)* distance between voices.

 a) Range—Each of the four voices should, as a rule, be written in the normal singing range of that voice.

Fig. 5.3.

    soprano   alto   tenor   bass

Voices ordinarily should be kept within the ranges outlined by the whole notes. Pitches outside of these ranges are possible, but should be used only sparingly and within the limits of the black notes.

 b) Doubling—Since four notes will be used, one note of the triad must be doubled, that is, two voices will have to use the same letter name, either in unison or in an octave relationship. The root of the triad is usually doubled.

Fig. 5.4.

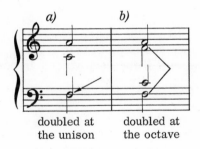

     doubled at doubled at
     the unison the octave

 c) Position—Triads may appear in either of two positions, open or close. In *open position*[2] the distance between the soprano and tenor is an octave or more; in *close position*, the distance between the soprano and tenor is less than an octave. In either position, any interval may appear between tenor and bass.

---

[2]The terms *open structure* and *close structure* are commonly used synonymously with *open position* and *close position*.

Fig. 5.5.

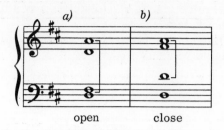

Note also that in open position another note of the triad could be in-serted between the tenor and the soprano, while in close position, the three upper voices are as close together as possible.

d) *Distance between voices* —The distance between any two adjacent voices (for example, soprano and alto) usually does not ex-ceed an octave, except that an interval larger than an octave may appear between the bass and tenor voices.

Voices should not be crossed, that is, the alto should not be low-er than the tenor, the tenor should not be lower than the bass, and so on.

WRITTEN MATERIALS

Assignment 15. Fill in the inner voices of each triad in both close position and open position, in that order. At present use two roots, one third and one fifth; keep voices in correct pitch range. Here is an example.

Fig. 5.6.

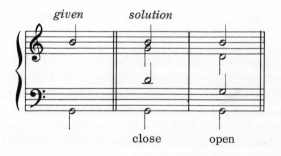

The given note on the bass staff is always the root of a major triad.

Assignment 16. Write each of the following triads on the staff in both close and open position. The bass will carry the root of the triad in all cases. Observe doubling and voice range instructions as given in Assignment 15. The number after the triad indicates the soprano note to be used (Example G♭(3)).

Fig. 5.7.

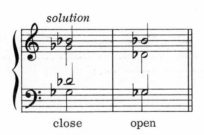

close   open

G (3), D (5), E (3), C♯(5), D♭ (1), B (1), C♭ (1), D♯(5), A♭ (3), F♯(3).

The Connection of Repeated Triads

Part-Writing Rule No. 1 (Repeated Triads with Roots in Bass).[3] When two triads, each with the same spelling, are used in succession, both triads may be written in the same position, or each may be in a different position.

Several factors determine which method will be used.

a) The necessity of keeping voices in a good register. In the example, continuing close position *a)* places both tenor and alto in excessively high ranges. Changing the position *b)* corrects this situation.

---

[3] Rule numbers do not appear consecutively in the text. Rules are numbered to provide maximum ease of reference in Appendix 1.

Fig. 5.8.

b) Avoidance of large leaps (fifths or larger) in the inner voices. In the example, maintaining the same position *a)* causes large leaps in the tenor and alto. Changing the position *b)* corrects this situation.

Fig. 5.9.

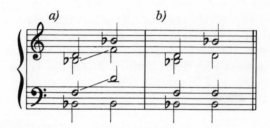

c) The necessity to maintain correct voice distribution (two roots, one third and one fifth). Maintaining the same position *a)* makes it impossible to keep the correct chord distribution. Changing the position *b)* corrects this situation.

Fig. 5.10.

(no 5th)

Often either solution is correct. In the following example, changing position *a)* is correct; maintaining the same position *b)* is also correct.

Fig. 5.11.

Assignment 17. Choose the better of the two solutions in each of
the pairs of examples. Explain why you made your choice. State if
both solutions are correct.

Assignment 18. Write each pair of repeated triads using whichever method is more appropriate.

In writing successive positions of the same chord, the following observations may be helpful.

a) When maintaining the same position, move all three upper voices in the same direction.

Fig. 5.12.

b) When changing position, two voices (the bass and one other) remain stationary, while the other two voices exchange tones.

Fig. 5.13.

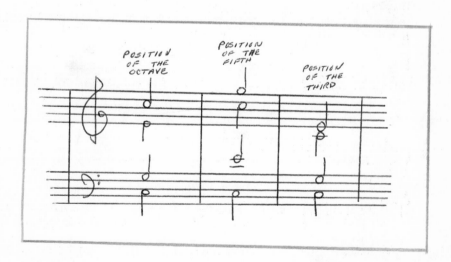

The Minor Triad;
The Melodic Line in Minor

THEORY AND ANALYSIS

The Minor Triad

Of the four types of triads, the minor triad, in its frequency of usage, ranks in importance with the major triad. In common with the major triad, it encompasses the distance of a perfect fifth from the root to the fifth of the triad. The triads differ in that the two thirds are reversed—in the minor triad the interval from the root to the third is a minor third; the interval from the third to the fifth is a major third.

Fig. 6.1.

a) Major triad: *b)* Minor triad:

P5   M3   m3   P5   m3   M3

Minor Triad Spelling

With a knowledge of interval names and spellings, the minor triad may be spelled by interval. These are the intervals in the minor triad.

1 up to 3	Minor Third (m3)	3 down to 1
3 up to 5	Major Third (M3)	5 down to 3
5 up to 1	Perfect Fourth (P4)	1 down to 5

58

1 up to 5	Perfect Fifth (P5)	5 down to 1
3 up to 1	Major Sixth (M6)	1 down to 3
5 up to 3	Minor Sixth (m6)	3 down to 5
1 up to 1 ⎫		⎧ 1 down to 1
3 up to 3 ⎬	Perfect Octave (P8)	⎨ 3 down to 3
5 up to 5 ⎭		⎩ 5 down to 5

Assignment 19. Minor triad spelling.

   a) Spell with letter names the minor triad when each of the following is the root.   D, A, C, F, E♭, A♭, G♯, B, G♭, B♭.

   b) Spell the minor triad when each of the following is the third.   F, C, B♭, E, E♭, D, F♯, G♯, A, B, D♭.

   c) Spell the minor triad when each of the following is the fifth. A, B, D, G, F♯, B♭, C♯, A♭, F, D♯.

   Assignment 20. Based on a given triad, spell each of the intervals in the table of intervals.   Example: C♯ minor triad.

m3	C♯ up to E		m6	G♯ up to E
M3	E up to G♯		M6	E up to C♯
P4	G♯ up to C♯		P8	C♯ up to C♯
P5	C♯ up to G♯			E up to E
				G♯ up to G♯

Do the same with minor triads as assigned.

   Assignment 21. Identify intervals from minor triads in melodies 12, 21, 24, 27, 36, 41 and 53 from Part I of *Music for Sight Singing.* Follow example of Assignment 4.

The Melodic Line in Minor

   As its name implies, the melodic form of the minor scale is generally used in melodic writing. When a melody line ascends from the dominant note to the tonic note through the sixth and seventh scale steps, these scale steps are usually raised.

Fig. 6.2.

When the melody descends from tonic to dominant through the seventh and sixth scale steps, these scale steps are usually lowered.

Fig. 6.3.

When either the sixth or seventh scale step is used without the other in a step-wise passage, the seventh scale step is raised and proceeds up (Figure 6.4. *a*) and the sixth scale step is lowered and proceeds down (Figure 6.5. *a*). When both are used, but do not proceed between dominant and tonic, or the reverse, the direction in which the last note of the group proceeds determines the form of the scale (ascending or descending) to be used. (Figures 6.4*b* and 6.5*b*.)

Fig. 6.4. 7 proceeds up

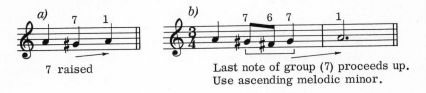

7 raised

Last note of group (7) proceeds up.
Use ascending melodic minor.

Fig. 6.5. 6 proceeds down

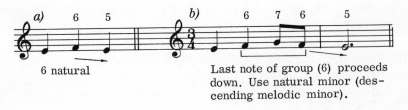

6 natural

Last note of group (6) proceeds down. Use natural minor (descending melodic minor).

Fig. 6.6.

Assignment 22. Analyze melodies in a minor key. These melodies from *Music for Sight Singing* contain examples of scale-wise passages including the sixth and/or seventh scale steps: Part I, Numbers 21, 196, 212; Part II, Numbers 11, 39.   Locate these

passages (in Number 21, measures 1, 6-7, 10) and describe the use of the sixth and seventh scale steps.

Figured Bass (*used mainly in 17th & 18th cent.*)

In the late sixteenth century, a procedure was devised whereby the structure of a chord was determined by reading Arabic numerals found under the bass line of a composition. This procedure, in which each Arabic numeral indicates an interval above the bass note, is known as *figured bass* or *thorough bass*.

In Figure 6.7, the $\frac{5}{3}$ indicates that the interval of a third and the interval of a fifth should be placed above the bass note G (the G in the soprano results from normal doubling and is usually not noted in the figuration). Thus, $\frac{5}{3}$ usually indicates that the bass note is the root of a triad.

Fig. 6.7.

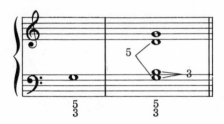

In actual practice, when the bass note is the root of a triad, the $\frac{5}{3}$, although it is not written, is usually understood to be below the bass note. If one or more of the notes above the bass require an accidental, then those numbers only, with accidentals, appear. An accidental used without a number always refers to the third above the bass note. A slash through a number means the same as a sharp before a number.

Fig. 6.8.

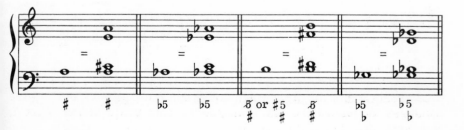

Figured bass does not indicate open or close structure, nor does it indicate soprano position. All possible arrangements of a triad with the root in the bass will be served by the same figured bass symbol.

Fig. 6.9.

With a key signature, the figured bass calls for that letter name above the bass indicated by the signature. A ♮ (natural sign) is used to cancel out an unwanted chromatic in the key signature.

Fig. 6.10.

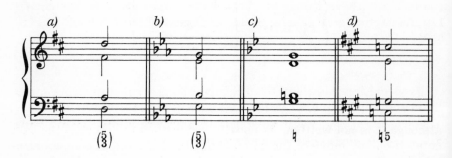

Minor triads (or any other type of chord) can be indicated by figured bass.

Fig. 6.11.

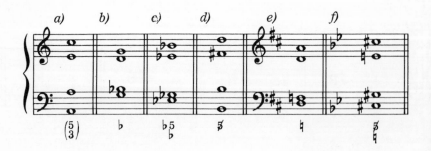

Most important to remember about figured bass is that the Arabic numeral below the bass note indicates the *interval above the bass part*.

APPLICATION

WRITTEN MATERIALS

Minor Triads

Assignment 23. Write minor triads on the staff. Refer to Assignment 19. Write each triad listed in Assignment 19 in the treble and bass clef, as shown in Figure 2.3.

Assignment 24. Write intervals from the minor triad on the staff, referring to Assignment 20. Place each interval, ascending and descending, on the treble or bass clef, as assigned, and as shown in Figure 2.4

Melody Writing

Assignment 25. Write melodies in minor keys in either simple or compound time, as assigned. Follow directions given in Assignment 12. Be particularly careful of the treatment of the sixth and seventh scale steps.

Part-Writing

Part-writing the minor triad involves no new rules or procedures. Follow all directions for part-writing as given in Chapter 5.

Assignment 26. Write each pair of repeated minor triads, using whichever method is more appropriate.

Assignment 27. Write pairs of repeated triads when no key signature is given. Determine from the figured bass whether the triad is major or minor.

Fig. 6.12. Example.

Assignment 27.

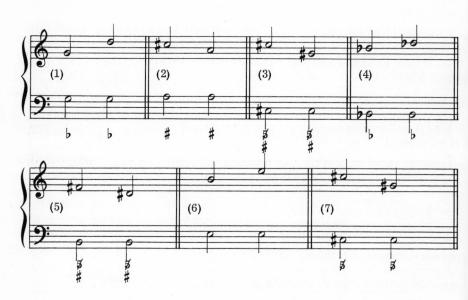

Assignment 28. Write pairs of repeated triads when key signature is given. The figured bass will determine whether the triad is major or minor.

Fig. 6.13. Example.

Assignment 28.

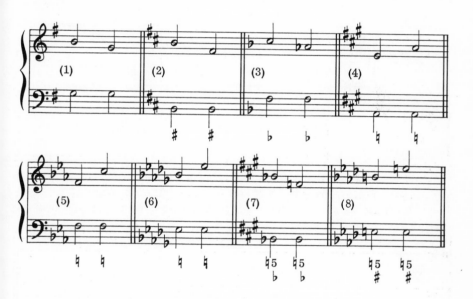

EAR TRAINING AND MUSIC READING

The Minor Triad

Exercise 36. Singing the minor triad: *a*) listen to minor triads played at the piano. After each triad is sounded, sing the pattern 1-3-5-3-1.

b) Listen to the triad. Sing the root of the triad only.

Exercise 37. *a*) Play or listen to any given pitch. Call this pitch "1." Sing a minor triad from this pitch.

b) Call the given pitch "5." Sing the triad pattern.

c) Call the given pitch "3." Sing the triad pattern.

Exercise 38. Repeat Exercise 37. Instead of singing with numbers, sing with triad spellings.

Exercise 39. *a)* Repeat Exercise 37, but be prepared to sing either a major or minor triad as directed by instructor.

b) Repeat Exercise 38, but be prepared to sing either a major or minor triad with triad spellings.

Exercise 40. *a)* Identify the soprano note of a minor triad as 1, 3 or 5 of the triad when the triad is played at the piano.

b) Listen to a series of major and minor triads, mixed. Identify the soprano note and indicate whether the triad is major or minor. For example, the answers to the examples below would be 5M, 3m, 1m, 3M (M = major, m = minor).

Fig. 6.14.

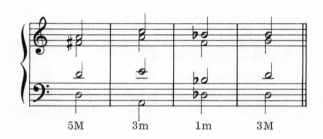

Exercise 41. *a)* Spell a minor triad when the triad is played at the piano. Follow directions given for Exercise 12 (page 23).

b) Same as *a)*, but triads played will be both major and minor, mixed.

Exercises 36 through 41 can be practiced by students working in pairs. Review directions as given on page 25.

Intervals in the Minor Triad

Intervals in the minor triad are a different arrangement of those in the major triad. The problem in singing or recognizing intervals from minor triads is to use these familiar intervals in their new context.

Exercises 42-45. Repeat Exercises 13-16 (pages 24-25), but base the exercises upon minor triads rather than major triads.

Exercise 46. Repeat Exercise 18 (page 25), basing the exercise upon minor triads rather than major triads.

Sight Singing

Melodies in minor keys from Chapters 1 and 2 of *Music for Sight Singing* can now be used for sight singing practice. The use of the natural minor scale in melodic writing is virtually indistinguishable from the Aeolian mode (see Chapter 17, *Music for Sight Singing*). One example of the natural minor scale is presented at this point, melody Number 53 in Chapter 2. Use of the harmonic minor scale will not be found because of the presence of the augmented second interval.

Melodic Dictation

Exercise 47. Taking melodic dictation in minor keys. Follow directions given for melodic dictation on pages 47-48. When listening to melodies in a minor key, pay particular attention to the use of the sixth and seventh scale degrees. The melodies you hear will *usually* conform to the rules given in the discussion of melody writing. Melodies will contain skips in the tonic triad only, and may be in either simple or compound time.

KEYBOARD HARMONY

Exercise 48. Play the minor triad with the root in the bass in each of its three soprano positions. Follow directions given for playing the major triad (Exercise 19, page 26).

Exercise 49. Play Assignments 26-28 at the keyboard.

7

The Three Principal Triads of the Key; Tonic and Dominant Harmonies

THEORY AND ANALYSIS

The tonic, subdominant and dominant triads are often known as the three principal triads of a key.

E Major			E	G#	B				I	
	A	C#	E		B	D#	F#		IV	V

C Minor			C	Eb	G				i	
	F	Ab	C		G	Bb	D		iv	v

In a minor key, the three principal minor triads contain the scale degrees of the natural (pure) minor scale. Alteration of the sixth and seventh scale steps will change one or both of the triads.

C minor harmonic form			C	Eb	G			i	
	F	Ab	C		G	B	D	iv	V

Dominant triad is major (V)

C minor, melodic form			C	Eb	G			i	
	F	A	C		G	B	D	IV	V

Subdominant and dominant triads are major (IV and V)

Assignment 29. a) Spell the three principal triads in each major key.

b) Spell the three principal triads in each minor key. These should be spelled for each of three scale forms.

The Harmonic Cadence: Authentic Cadences

The nature and use of the cadence has already been studied on page 21. It was observed that the melodic cadence is a point in a melody at which a musical idea seems to end and that a chord succession at such a point is a harmonic cadence. The most common cadence progressions are those using the three principal triads of the key (I, IV, V). The three cadences composed of the dominant and tonic triads are known as *authentic cadences*.

a) The *perfect authentic cadence*—the progression V-I in which the V triad has the root in the bass and the final I triad has the root in both bass and soprano.

The soprano line usually proceeds from leading tone to tonic (7-1), or supertonic to tonic (2-1). (See Figure 7.1 *a* and *b*)

b) The *imperfect authentic cadence*—the progression V-I in which the final I triad is found with some note other than the root in either soprano or bass.

The commonly used soprano lines are 2-3 and 5-5 (see Figure 7.1 *c* and *d*). Figure 7.1 *e* illustrates an authentic imperfect cadence with the leap 5 down to 3 in the soprano.

c) The *authentic half cadence*—the progression I-V. (See Figure 7.1 *f, g, h, i*)

Fig. 7.1.[1]

---

[1]In this and subsequent figures, major keys are identified by capital letters, minor keys by lower case letters. F = F major; f = f minor.

In a minor key, the dominant triad in the cadence is usually a major triad (for example, in c minor, V-i; G B D, C E♭ G). In music of the sixteenth, seventeenth and early eighteenth centuries, the major triad was considered more consonant than the minor triad, hence it is common to find the final tonic triad in a minor key altered to become a major triad. This is known as a "picardy third" or "tierce de Picardie."

Fig. 7.2.

Fig. 7.3.   Bach, *Das neugeborne Kindelein* (#53)[2]

Assignment 30. Analysis of cadences in Bach chorales. From the "371 Chorales" by J. S. Bach, copy out the cadence triads from the chorale phrases listed below. Place chord numbers (I, IV, V; i, iv, v) under each triad and name the cadence (perfect authentic, imperfect authentic, and so on).

---

[2]In this and subsequent examples from the chorales by J. S. Bach, the number in parenthesis refers to the number of the chorale as found in the various published editions of the 371 chorales.

Fig. 7.4.   Bach, *Ich steh an deiner Krippen hier*

Authentic imperfect

Copy out the cadence triads of each of the following chorale phrases. In the chorales, the end of each phrase is marked by a *fermata* ($\frown$). Repeats in the chorales are not considered in the phrase numberings of this assignment.

Chorale No.	1 first phrase	42 second phrase
	8 final phrase	53 first phrase
	11 second phrase	98 final phrase
	12 third phrase	

Melodic Use of the Dominant (V) Triad

Intervals from the V triad are commonly used in melodic writing. Melodies 56-79 from Chapter 3 of *Music for Sight Singing* display intervals from the V triad.

Fig. 7.5.   German Folk Song (MSS I-57)

Assignment 31. Copy out melodies from Chapter 3 as assigned. Locate intervals in the dominant triad as shown in Figure 7.5.

Melodic Use of the Dominant Seventh (V^7) Chord[3]

A seventh chord is a four-note chord. A fourth note is added above a triad at the interval of a third above the fifth of the triad. It

---

[3]Because of the extensive melodic use of intervals from the V^7 chord, the melodic use of the V^7 chord is introduced at this point. Discussion of other uses of the V^7 chord will be found in Chapter 20.

is called a seventh chord because of the interval of a seventh above the root of the chord.

The seventh chord built upon the dominant tone of the key consists of the dominant triad plus the interval of a minor third above the fifth of the triad. The intervals found in this chord are frequently used in melodic writing.

Fig. 7.6.

Fig. 7.7.

(not common)

Assignment 32. Spell the V⁷ chord in each major or minor key.

Intervals: The intervals in the list below are from the dominant seventh chord and are those in which the seventh of the chord is involved. The underlined intervals are those most commonly used in melodic writing.

1 up to 7	minor seventh	7 down to 1
3 up to 7	diminished fifth⁴ (TRITONE)	7 down to 3
5 up to 7	minor third	7 down to 5
7 up to 1	major second	1 down to 7
7 up to 3	augmented fourth⁴ (TRITONE)	3 down to 7
7 up to 5	major sixth	5 down to 7

Fig. 7.8.

⁴Also known as a "tritone." See Chapter 14.

Assignment 33. Spell each of the intervals in Figure 7.8 based on the dominant seventh chord of any major or minor key.

Assignment 34. Melodic Analysis. From *Music for Sight Singing,* Chapter 3, melodies 80-98, copy out melodies as assigned and iden- tify those intervals found in the V^7 chord. Note that the seventh of the V^7 chord will be the fourth scale step. The interval of a minor third (5 up to 7, or 7 down to 5) is very commonly used.

Fig. 7.9.   American Folk Song (Kentucky) (MSS I-81)

APPLICATION

WRITTEN MATERIALS

Melody Writing

In a melodic line the leading tone of the key (the third of the V triad) may descend when it is found in a group of tones which out- lines all or part of the V triad (see Figure 7.5). When the descend- ing interval between the leading tone and the dominant is filled in as a scale-wise passage, there results a descending melodic line #7 - #6 - 5 as in Figure 7.10. The melodic line then usually pro- gresses by leap up to a member of the tonic triad. See also *Music for Sight Singing,* Part II - 59.

Fig. 7.10.   Johann Crüger (1640) *Herzliebster Jesu*

Assignment 35. Write melodies in phrases or periods as assigned, using intervals in the tonic and dominant triads.

While observing, singing or listening to intervals in the V^7 chord, note the special property of the seventh of the chord. It almost al- ways proceeds downwards, either to the scale step below or to another member of the V^7 chord.

Fig. 7.11.   German Folk Song (MSS I-80)

7 down by step

American Folk Song (Ohio) (MSS I-97)

7 down by skip in
same chord

In rare cases where the seventh is allowed to ascend, the melodic
line usually descends immediately after to effect a normal resolution of the seventh.

Fig. 7.12.   French Folk Song (MSS I-96)

resolution of 7 delayed

Assignment 36. Write melodic lines using intervals in the V^7
chord in keys and forms as assigned. Be particularly careful of the
resolution of the seventh of the V^7 chord.

Writing the Authentic Cadence

In previous part-writing exercises, the bass note remained stationary while the upper voices moved. In part-writing cadences, the
bass line moves, requiring the employment of new part-writing
techniques.

The cadences illustrated on pages 69-70 or those copied out for
Assignment 30 show that the roots of the two triads of the cadence
are always the interval of a fifth apart (or the inversion of the fifth,
the fourth).

Fig. 7.13.

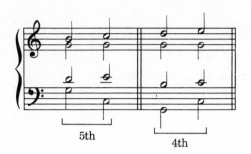

> 5th   4th

Part-Writing Rule 2A. (Triads with roots in the bass a fifth apart) In a progression of two triads whose roots in the bass line are a fifth apart, retain the common tone in the same voice and move the other voices step-wise.

Fig. 7.14.   Fig. 7.15.

common tone "g" in
alto; soprano and tenor
move stepwise

common tone "B^b" in
soprano; alto and tenor
move stepwise.

Assignment 37. Writing authentic cadences. Identify each as perfect, imperfect or half cadence.

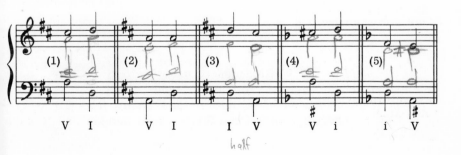

half

Since it is occasionally impossible to follow Rule 2A when writing two triads with their roots a fifth apart, there must be an alternate method.

Part-Writing Rule 2B. (Triads with roots in the bass a fifth apart) In a progression of two triads whose roots in the bass line are a fifth apart, move the three upper voices in similar motion to the nearest tones of the next triad.

Rule 2B is particularly valuable in the authentic cadence when the melody line is supertonic to tonic (2-1) or reverse, or when there is a leap in the melody.

Fig. 7.16.

By following Rule 2A, the second triad is left without a third. | Examples of correct use of Rule 2B.

Assignment 38. *a*) Write cadences using Rule 2B. Choose open or close structure according to needs of voice range.

b) Write cadences using either Rule 2A or Rule 2B as required by part-writing situation. Write chord number below each bass note.

Assignment 39. Write any or all of the following cadences in major or minor keys as assigned.

 a) The two perfect authentic cadences (soprano line 7-8 and 2-1).

 b) The imperfect authentic cadence in two positions (2-3, 5-5).

 c) The authentic half cadence in four positions (1-7, 1-2, 3-2, 5-5).

EAR TRAINING AND MUSIC READING

The Dominant Triad

Exercise 50. Singing the V triad in a major key.

 a) You will hear the tonic note of a major key played at the piano. Sing the tonic triad, using letter names. The fifth of the tonic triad is the root of the V triad. From this note sing the V triad, using letter names.

Fig. 7.17.

 b) Sing the V triad without first singing the I triad.

Exercise 51. Singing the V triad in a minor key. Follow the same procedure as Exercise 50. The i triad will be minor, the V triad will be major. The minor dominant triad (v) will not be considered at this time. (See Chapter 18.)

Fig. 7.18.

Harmonic Dictation

In harmonic dictation, the student is asked to identify the function (chord number) of each of a series of chords while listening to those chords.

Exercise 52. a) Identify authentic cadences when played. Listen to a phrase of music played at the piano.

    1) At the conclusion of the first playing, sing the tonic of the key.

    2) During the second playing, sing the roots of the cadence chords.

    3) During the third playing, sing the soprano line and identify the cadence as perfect or imperfect, or as a half cadence.

Fig. 7.19.

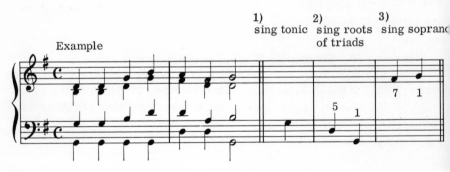

With continued practice, identify cadence completely in two hearings, and then in one hearing.

    b) Write the cadence from dictation on staff paper. The key or key signature will be given. Follow previous directions and in addition place soprano and bass notes on the staff. Fill in inner parts according to part-writing rules and identify cadence by name.

Sight Singing: In *Music for Sight Singing,* study page 19, followed by practice in sight singing from Chapter 3, sections *a*, *b* and *c*.

Exercise 53. Melodic dictation. Listen to melodies containing skips in the V triad and the I triad. Follow directions for melodic dictation as outlined on pages 47-48. In addition to these directions, when the name of the key becomes known, spell the I and V triads, and sing them if so directed.

The Dominant Seventh Chord

Exercise 54. Singing the V^7 chord. Sing a V triad as in Exercises 50-51, but add a minor third above the fifth of the triad to create the V^7 chord. Sing the chord with letter names in all major and minor keys.

Exercise 55. Sing intervals from the V^7 chord, as directed.

Sight Singing: Practice singing melodies from Chapter 3, section *d*, of *Music for Sight Singing*. Follow this with Chapter 4, which contains examples of intervals in both the V triad and the V^7 chord in melodies written in compound time.

Exercise 56. Melodic dictation. Dictation exercises will now contain intervals from the V triad and the V^7 chord.

KEYBOARD HARMONY

Exercise 57. Playing cadences at the keyboard.

a) Play the perfect authentic cadence (soprano line 7-8) in all keys, major and minor. When playing the cadence, the part-writing rules should be observed. For convenience, the cadences may be played in close position, with the right hand playing the three upper tones of the triad.

Fig. 7.20.

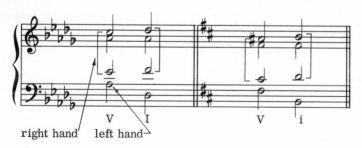

For practice, use the circle of keys. Start at any key and proceed around the circle until you arrive at the key from which you started.

b) Play the perfect authentic cadence, soprano line (2-1), in all keys, major and minor.

c) Play the imperfect authentic cadence in all keys, major and minor.

d) Play the authentic half cadence in all keys, major and minor.

Exercise 58. Play at the keyboard the cadences in Assignments 37 and 38.

Exercise 59. Harmonize melodic cadences at the piano. Play a given melody at the piano. At the point of a melodic cadence, harmonize the cadence using the cadence formulas studied in Exercise 57. Practice Figure 7.21.

Figure 7.21.   Haydn: Canon (MSS I-12)

r.h.

l.h.   V   i

Perfect Authentic Cadence

Apply the same procedure to the following melodies from Part I of *Music for Sight Singing*.

8, 24(4), 25, 32(2,4), 38, 47, 101(1,2,4), 109

Play a cadence at the end of each phrase mark, by harmonizing the last two notes of the melody at that point. Where a number in parentheses above follows a melody number, play the entire melody but play cadences only at the end of phrase marks indicated. In melody 32, for example, play the entire melody, but play cadence at the end of the second and fourth phrase marks.

When a melody appears in the bass clef, play it one octave higher than written.

8

The Alto and Tenor Clefs

THEORY AND ANALYSIS

The C clef is universally used in music, though not as commonly as the treble and bass clefs. The C clef sign ▯ or ▯ indicates the location of *middle c* on the staff. It is particularly useful for those instruments whose range extends from the middle part of the bass clef to the middle of the treble clef.

Fig. 8.1.

Fig. 8.2.

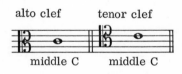

alto clef   tenor clef

middle C   middle C

When the C clef is found on the third line of the staff, it is known as the *alto clef,* used by the viola and by the trombone. When the C clef is found on the fourth line of the staff, it is known as the *tenor clef,* and is often used by the violoncello, the bassoon, the trombone, and occasionally by the double bass. Illustrations of actual usages of these clefs can be found in Figures 8.3-8.5.

Fig. 8.3.

Beethoven, Quartet, Op. 18, No. 1
first movement

Fig. 8.4.

Dvořák, Concerto for Violoncello and Orchestr
in B minor, Op. 104, second mvt.

Fig. 8.5.   Tschaikowski, Symphony No. 6, third mvt.

These two clefs, together with the treble and bass clefs, are the only ones remaining in common use today from a system of ten different clef signs used in music before 1750. The other six clefs are seen in Figure 8.6.

Fig. 8.6.

These clefs can be found in very old editions of music and in many modern publications of pre-nineteenth century music.

Exercise 60. a) Learn the names of the lines and spaces of the alto clef. Be able to name any line or space correctly, for example, name the fourth line—answer, E. In addition, be able to locate any pitch name in the alto clef.

b) Learn the names of the lines and spaces of the tenor clef, as above.

Sharps and flats for the key signatures are placed as follows on the alto and tenor clefs.

Fig. 8.7.

Assignment 40. Write the signature for each major and minor key in both the alto and tenor clefs.

APPLICATION

EAR TRAINING AND MUSIC READING

Sight Singing: Sing melodies from Chapter 5 in *Music for Sight Singing.* To facilitate the learning of these clefs, the student should sing the letter name of each note (do not sing the word sharp or flat). Study methods of clef transposition discussed at the beginning of Chapter 5 of *Music for Sight Singing* and apply to melodies from Chapters 1-4.

Exercise 61. Melodic dictation. Dictation exercises will now be given in the alto and tenor clef. Remember that " C" in these clefs is middle C; be careful not to write your solution an octave too high or too low.

The Subdominant Triad;
Plagal Cadences

9

THEORY AND ANALYSIS

The subdominant triad in a major key is a major triad (IV). In a minor key it may be either minor (iv) or major (IV). Of the two, the iv triad is the most usual. The IV triad is sometimes necessary when the raised sixth scale degree in a melodic line occurs simultaneously with a subdominant triad in the harmony.

Fig. 9.1. iv in minor   Bach, *Wo soll ich fliehen hin* (#281)

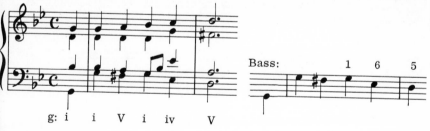

Fig. 9.2. IV in minor   Anon. (c.1670) *Nun sich der Tag geendet hat*

85

Melodic Use of the Subdominant Triad

Intervals from the subdominant triad are used in melodic writing though less frequently than intervals from the tonic and dominant triads.

Fig. 9.3.   Memel Folk Song (MSS I-142)

A: (IV=DF#A)   IV

Assignment 41. Copy out melodies from the following list, found in Chapters 6-7 of Music for Sight Singing, as assigned. Indicate the location of intervals from the subdominant triad.   Part I, Numbers 144, 145, 151, 153, 157, 163, 170, 173.

The Plagal Cadence

Cadences composed of the subdominant and tonic triads are known as plagal cadences.   Although it is not used as frequently as the authentic cadence, the plagal cadence is familiar through its use as the " Amen" following most hymns.

Fig. 9.4.   Hymn: St. Anne[1]

A - men.

IV   I

The plagal cadence is found in the same three forms as was the authentic cadence.

a) The *perfect plagal cadence*—the progression IV-I in which the IV triad has the root in the bass and the final I triad has the root

---

[1]"St. Anne" is the name of the hymn tune. A hymn is often found in different hymnals with different words, but the name of the tune will always be the same. It can be located in an "Index of Tunes" found in most hymnals. St. Anne is commonly known using the texts "O where are kings and empires now" and "O God, our help in ages past."   In this text, hymns will be identified by the name of the hymn tune.

in both bass and soprano. (See Figure 9.5 *a*)

b) The *imperfect plagal cadence*—the progression IV-I in which the final I triad is found with some other note than the root in either soprano or bass. (See Figure 9.5 *b*, *c* and *d*)

c) The *plagal half cadence*—the progression I-IV (not common). (See Figure 9.5 *e*, *f* and *g*)

Fig. 9.5.

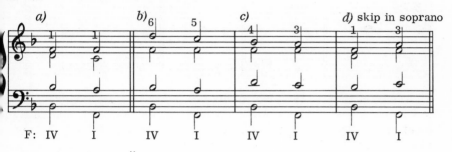

F: IV   I   IV   I   IV   I   IV   I

perfect plagal ‖ imperfect plagal

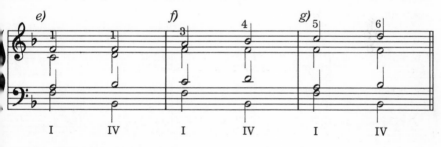

I   IV   I   IV   I   IV

plagal half (not common)

APPLICATION

WRITTEN MATERIALS

Melody Writing

Assignment 42. Write melodies in phrases or periods as assigned, using intervals in the tonic, dominant and subdominant triads. Intervals in the subdominant triad should be used infrequently in comparison with the frequency of intervals in the tonic and dominant triads.

Writing the Plagal Cadence

Most plagal cadences, illustrated in Figure 9.5, can be written using part-writing Rule 2A. In each plagal cadence the roots of the

two triads are a fifth (fourth) apart.   Plagal cadences in which there
is a leap in the melody can be written using Rule 2B. (See Figure
9.5 *d*)

Assignment 43. Writing plagal cadences. Fill in alto and tenor
voices. Identify each cadence as perfect or imperfect.

Assignment 44. Writing authentic and plagal cadences. Fill in
inner voices. Write chord number below each bass note. Identify
each cadence by name.

Assignment 45. Write the following cadences in major or minor keys, as assigned.

a) The perfect plagal cadence (1-1).

b) The imperfect plagal cadence in two positions (6-5, 4-3).

c) The plagal half cadence in three positions (1-1, 3-4, 5-6).

Assignment 46. *a*) Part write cadences when bass line only is given. Supply any correct soprano line.

b) Part write cadences when soprano line only is given. Be sure the bass note is always the root of the triad.

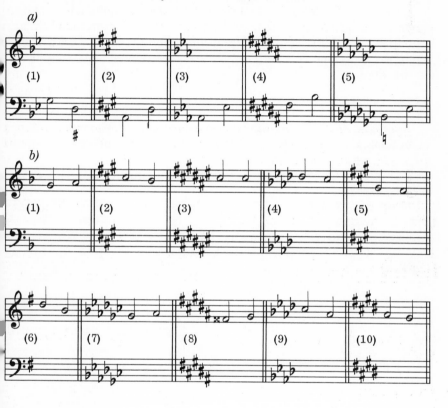

a)

(1)   (2)   (3)   (4)   (5)

b)

(1)   (2)   (3)   (4)   (5)

(6)   (7)   (8)   (9)   (10)

AR TRAINING AND MUSIC READING

Exercise 62.   Singing the IV triad in a major key.

a) You will hear the tonic note of a major key. Sing the tonic triad with letter names. The root of the IV triad is found a perfect fourth above the tonic. Sing this interval; then sing the IV triad with letter names.

b) Sing the IV triad after hearing the tonic note, but without singing the tonic triad.

Exercise 63. Singing the iv triad in a minor key.
  a) Follow the same procedure as in the preceding exercise.
  b) Sing the IV triad in a minor key, as above.

Exercise 64. Harmonic Dictation. *a)* Identify plagal cadences when played. Follow directions given in Exercise 52.
  b) Write plagal cadences from dictation on staff paper. Follow directions given in Exercise 52.

Sight Singing. In *Music for Sight Singing,* study pages 46-47, followed by practice in sight singing from Chapters 6 and 7.

Exercise 65. Melodic dictation. Listen to melodies containing skips in the IV (or iv) triad. Follow directions for melodic dictation as outlined in Exercise 33. In addition, when the key becomes known spell the I, V and IV triads (or i, V and iv triads) and sing them i so directed.

KEYBOARD HARMONY

Exercise 66. Playing plagal cadences at the keyboard. Following directions given in Exercise 57, play each of the plagal cadences i all keys, major and minor.

Exercise 67. Play cadences from Assignments 43, 44 and 46 a the keyboard.

Exercise 68. Harmonizing melodic plagal cadences at the key board. Following directions given in Exercise 59, harmoniz cadences in the following melodies from Part I of *Music for Sigh Singing:* 1, 43 (third phrase mark, cadence is C - B$^\flat$), 99, 140, 14. (2, 4).

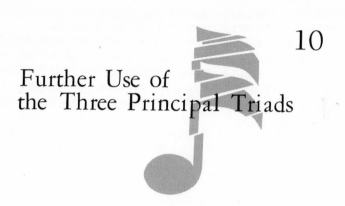

10

Further Use of
the Three Principal Triads

THEORY AND ANALYSIS

In addition to the triad progressions previously studied (V-I, IV-I, I-V, I-IV), the progression IV-V or iv-V may be used, either within the phrase or at the cadence. The progression V-IV (V-iv) is not commonly used.

Fig. 10.1.

Hymn: Toulon (Old 124th)

Fig. 10.2.

Coventry Carol, arr. Stainer

APPLICATION

WRITTEN MATERIALS

Writing the Progression IV-V

The roots of the IV and V triads are a second apart, so the progression IV-V cannot be written with part-writing rules already studied.

Part-Writing Rule 3. In a progression of two triads whose roots in the bass line are a second apart, move the three upper voices to the nearest triad tones in contrary motion to the bass. (See also Figures 10.1-10.2)

Fig. 10.3.

Violation of this rule is one of the most frequent causes of the appearance of three weaknesses in part-writing most likely to plague the beginning student. They are

 a) parallel perfect fifths.
 b) parallel octaves.
 c) the melodic augmented second.

Fig. 10.4.

The following examples show how violation of Rule 3 can cause the unwanted progressions.

Fig. 10.5.

The progression in Figure 10.5 *d* does not successfully avoid parallel octaves. In addition, the leap of a seventh in the bass line is poor melodic practice. The easiest way to avoid these "poor" progressions is to use the rules; when they are followed, it is impossible for the violations to appear.

Note, however, that octaves or fifths repeated on the same pitches are *not* considered parallel; the use of these "stationary" octaves or fifths is acceptable.

Fig. 10.6.

Most composers of the eighteenth and nineteenth centuries usually avoided the use of these progressions, particularly the parallel fifth and the parallel octave. They are to be considered incorrect in student work because they are not part of the historical style under study.

Parallel fifths and octaves are often a feature of the style of many twentieth-century composers. The melodic interval of the augmented second has been used in the nineteenth-century music suggestive of the Orient, since the interval is found in many Eastern scales. (See Figures 10.7-10.8.)   Such usages should be avoided by the elementary harmony student.

Fig. 10.7.   Ravel, *L'enfant et les Sortileges*

Fig. 10.8.   Saint-Saëns, *Samson and Delilah*

Assignment 47. Write cadences as found below. Write in chord numbers.

Assignment 48. Write, on staff paper, the progression I-IV-V-I or i-iv-V-i, in the following keys, or in other keys as assigned.

E♭ major	A♭ minor
B major	C♯ minor
F♯ major	F minor
D♭ major	D♯ minor

Exceptions to Part-Writing Rule 2

In a few special instances when chords are found with their roots a fifth apart, procedures other than those expressed by Rules 2A and 2B are used.

Part-Writing Rule 2C. In a progression of two triads whose roots in the bass line are a fifth apart, move the third of the first triad to the third of the second triad, hold the common tone, and move the other voice step-wise.

Fig. 10.9.

This rule has three principal uses, as illustrated in Figures 10.9-10.12.

  a) to change position, open to close, when the skip from third to third is in the tenor (Figures 10.9 a, 10.10).

  b) to change position, close to open, when the skip from third to third is in the soprano (Figures 10.9 b, 10.11).

  c) to give variety to the final cadence (Figure 10.12).

Fig. 10.10.   Brahms, *Die Wollust in den Maien*

Fig. 10.11.   Hymn: Capetown

Fig. 10.12.   Bach: *Du Lebensfürst, Herr Jesu Christ* (#361)

Part-Writing Rule 2D. In an authentic cadence, the root of the tonic triad may be tripled, omitting the fifth of the triad.

Fig. 10.13.

When, in a cadence (authentic), Rule 2A or Rule 2B seems to be called for, Rule 2D may be substituted when it is desirable that the leading tone of the key ascends to the tonic.

Fig. 10.14.   Hymn: Toulon

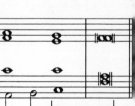

Assignment 49. Write cadences, using Rules 2C and 2D as indicated.

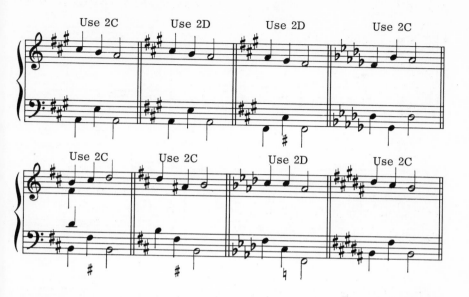

The triad progressions used in the study of the cadence can also be used in a longer succession of triads to form a phrase. Any pair of triads in the following assignments can be connected with Rules 1, 2A, B, C, D and 3.

Assignment 50. Fill in alto and tenor voices using part-writing procedures studied thus far. Make harmonic analysis by placing correct Roman numeral below each bass note.

Assignment 51. Supply soprano, alto and tenor lines above a given bass line. In writing a soprano line, observe the rules for melody writing previously studied, particularly the treatment of the leading tone. Make harmonic analysis.

Assignment 52. Harmonize melodies, supplying alto, tenor and bass parts. Follow this procedure.

a) Determine the key. Check not only the key signature, but sing melody through, observing the nature of the cadence to determine whether the melody is major or minor.

b) Write in the chord numbers for the cadence below the bass staff.

c) Write in chord numbers leading up to the cadence.

d) Write the bass line, each note being the root of the chosen chord.

e) Fill in inner parts.

EAR TRAINING AND MUSIC READING

Exercise 69. Extended exercises in harmonic dictation. As in part-writing, the harmonic progression used in the cadence can also be used in a harmonic dictation exercise of phrase length. Follow this procedure.

a) Listen to entire exercise without writing. At conclusion of exercise, sing the tonic.

b) On the second hearing, sing the root of each triad as the triad is played.

c) On the third hearing, sing the triad roots using the correct chord number.

d) Write the chord numbers.

As progress is made, eliminate steps *b)* and *c)*, at which time student may, after writing the chord numbers, write the soprano line and the bass line on the staff, as in melodic dictation. Inner parts can be filled in by following part-writing rules.

In this exercise, the progressions I-V, I-IV, V-I and IV-I will be used.

Exercise 70. Take harmonic dictation in which the chord progression IV-V or iv-V is used. Follow directions given in Exercise 69.

KEYBOARD HARMONY

Exercise 71. Playing the progression I IV V I at the keyboard. Play the progression with the I triad in each of its three possible soprano positions. Play in all major and minor keys. Follow all part-writing rules.

Fig. 10.15. Major Key:

I   IV   V   I

---

*Final I chord may be found with root in soprano by using Rule 2B in V I progression.

Fig. 10.16. Minor Key:

i   iv   V   i

Exercise 72. Melody harmonization at the keyboard. The melodies of Assignment 52 may be used at the keyboard. Play appropriate chord for each soprano note. For further practice, copy out each melody in various keys. Using melody (1) from Assignment 52 as an example, this can be done as follows:

  a) Note the key; in this case, B♭ major.
  b) Identify each soprano note by its scale number.

Fig. 10.17.

  c) Choose a new key, F for example. Write the melody in the new key by using the same scale numbers.

Fig. 10.18.

  d) Harmonize the melody in the key of F major at the piano.

11

The Triad in Inversion

THEORY AND ANALYSIS

A triad (or any chord) is said to be in *inversion* when some note other than the root is in the bass. When the third is in the bass the triad is in *first inversion;* when the fifth is in the bass, the triad is in *second inversion.* Since there are three possible soprano positions and three possible bass positions in a triad, a total of nine combinations of soprano and bass tones exists.

Fig. 11.1.

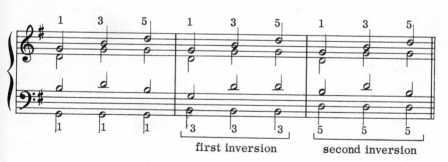

When figured bass is required, the symbol 6 is ordinarily used to indicate first inversion. The complete symbol is $\frac{6}{3}$, meaning that there can be found above the bass note an interval of a third and an interval of a sixth (Figure 11.2a). Generally, the 3 is omitted, but understood to be present (Figure 11.2b); if it is necessary to raise or lower the third above the bass, the symbols $\frac{6}{\sharp}$ or $\frac{6}{\flat}$ are used (Figure 11.2 c, d).

Fig. 11.2.

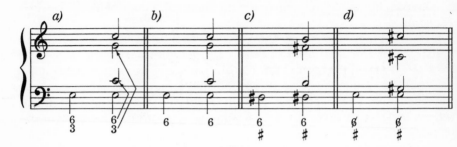

The figured bass symbol $\frac{6}{4}$ indicates second inversion. Neither number is omitted.

Fig. 11.3.

Inversion may be indicated in the Roman numeral chord designation by placing a figured bass symbol to the right and a little below the Roman numeral, 6 for first inversion and $\frac{6}{4}$ for second inversion. Examples: IV$_6$ = IV triad in first inversion; i$_6^{}$ = i triad in second inversion. When a figured bass symbol is used thus in conjunction with a Roman numeral, it is not necessary to include those chromatic indications which are necessary when the figured bass is found alone below a bass note. Given a specific key, the chord can be spelled by its Roman numeral designation; the figured bass symbol merely indicates in which inversion the chord is found. For example, see Figure 11.5, i$_6$. In the key of F minor, the figured bass is $\overset{\flat 6}{4}$ since $A^\flat$ is not in the key signature. The Roman numeral for analysis is $i_{\overset{6}{4}}$--in F minor, i is F $A^\flat$ C, and $\overset{6}{4}$ indicates that the triad is in second inversion.

Chords in inversion are found in musical compositions for two reasons.

    a) To give variety to the vertical sound. A composition consisting of chords with root in bass only is less interesting musically than alternation of chords with root in bass and chords in inversion.

    b) To allow the bass line to be more melodic. When roots in the bass only are used, the bass line will consist mostly of large intervals. Use of inversions allows more step-wise movement in the bass.

In Figure 11.4, the sign (*) locates examples of major triads in first inversion.

Fig. 11.4.   *Good King Wenceslas*

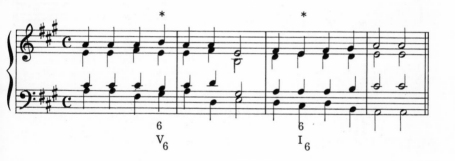

Triads in second inversion have a very limited use in the music of the eighteenth and nineteenth centuries. In contrast, there was very free use of the first inversion during this period. Only one of the possible uses of the triad in second inversion will be discussed in this chapter—the *accented cadential six-four chord.*

The cadential six-four chord is a tonic six-four chord found at the point of a cadence in a phrase of music and followed by V or V^7. It usually appears on the strong beat of the measure (Figure 11.5), although in triple meter it is often found on the second beat of the measure (Figure 11.6).

Fig. 11.5.   Handel, *Messiah*

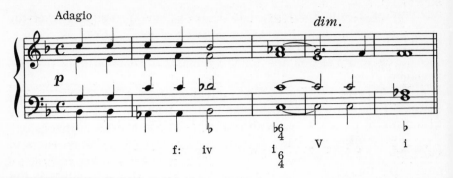

Fig. 11.6.   Hymn: St. Martin's

APPLICATION

WRITTEN MATERIALS

The Triad in First Inversion

New doubling procedures apply when the triad is found in inversion. In first inversion, normal procedure is to double the soprano note and to retain one each of the remaining triad members.

Fig. 11.7.

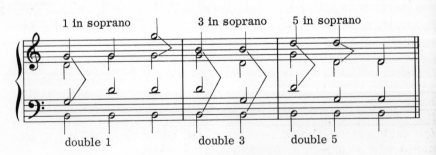

Assignment 53. a) Write single triads in first inversion when soprano and bass notes are given.

b) Write single triads when bass note only is given. Write each example in each of the three possible soprano positions.

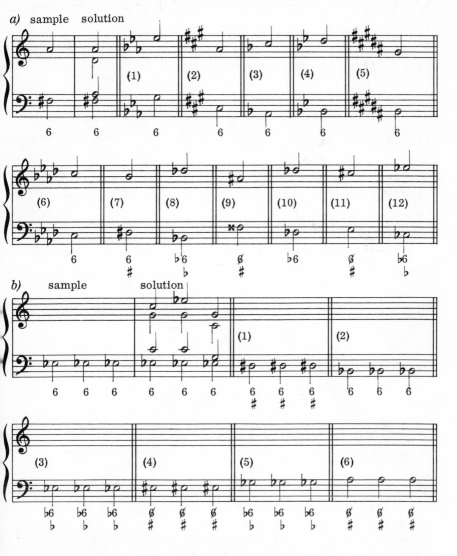

When writing from a triad in first inversion to the same triad with the root in the bass, or to a different triad with the root in the bass, the primary part-writing consideration is the correct resolution of the doubled note of the triad in first inversion. It is possible for such a pair of notes to move in one of three ways—by contrary motion, by oblique motion, or by similar motion.

Fig. 11.8.

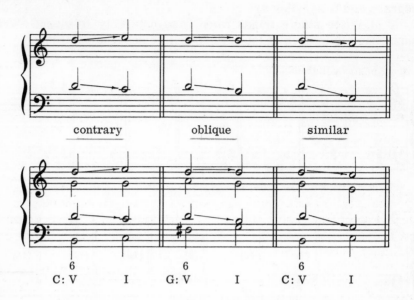

It is best to use contrary or oblique motion, using similar motion only when the other two types are impracticable or impossible. Usually, similar motion is necessary only in unusual cases where one voice must be brought into a better range.

Fig. 11.9.

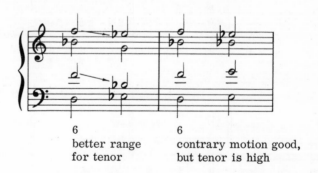

After writing the doubled note, there remains but one voice (besides the given bass) to move. Move this remaining voice to the nearest triad tone which will complete the triad with normal doubling. When the doubled note moves by oblique or contrary motion, the remaining voice usually moves by step or remains stationary, rarely moving by leap.

ig. 11.10.

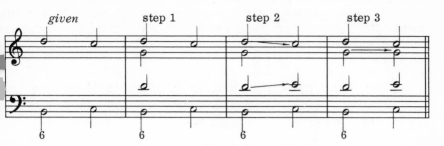

When writing from a triad with the root in the bass to a triad in
nversion, follow this same procedure. Write voices moving to the
oubled note first, using oblique or contrary motion when possible
nd filling in the remaining tone to complete the triad. Study ex-
mples in Figure 11.4.

Part-Writing Rule 6A.   When writing to or from a triad in first
nversion, write the two voices moving to or from the doubled note
irst, using contrary or oblique motion between the two voices, if
ossible. When using similar motion, care should be taken to avoid
arallel fifths and octaves.

Assignment 54. Write pairs of triads, following Rule 6A. As
sual, place chord numbers below each bass tone.

When triads in first inversion are used in succession, it is impossible for each of these triads to be found with normal doubling (soprano note doubled), since parallel octaves and fifths would result.

Fig. 11.11.

In this situation, each triad may have a different doubling if necessary.

Fig. 11.12.   Bach, *O Herre Gott, dein göttlich Wort* (#14)

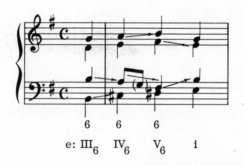

When using unusual doublings such as these, *avoid doubling the leading tone of the key, or any altered note* (such as the raised sixth scale step in minor). In the example above, Bach has succeeded in resolving each doubled note by contrary motion, has avoided doubling the raised sixth and seventh scale steps, and has moved from triad to triad with a minimum of motion. This example deserves careful study.

It is occasionally possible to double the soprano tone in each triad in successive first inversions, but the doubling occurs in different pairs of voices.

Fig. 11.13.

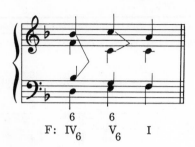

F: IV₆ V₆ I

Part-Writing Rule 6B. When first inversions of triads are found
in *succession,* each succeeding triad must either have a different
doubling or normal soprano doubling may appear in different pairs
of voices. Avoid doubling the leading tone or any altered tone.

Assignment 55. Write examples of successive first inversions
using Rule 6B.

The Triad in Second Inversion

When a triad is found in second inversion, the fifth of the triad
(the bass note) is usually doubled. (See Figures 11.5, 11.6, 11.14.)

In writing the accented cadential six-four chord, the bass note of
the I₆⁴ is usually approached by step-wise motion. Using triads

studied thus far, only the IV or IV₆ will precede the I₆⁴. Following the I_6^4, the interval of the sixth above the bass moves to the fift above the bass, while the fourth above the bass moves to the thir above the bass. (Exceptions will be noted in Chapter 18.)

Fig. 11.14.

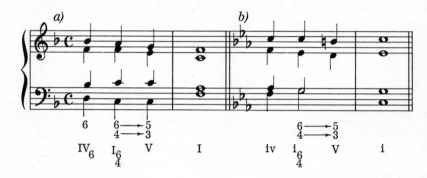

Assignment 56. Write examples of the accented cadential six four chord.

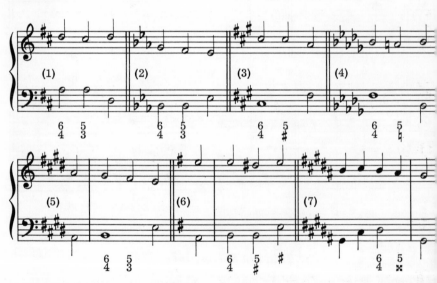

Assignment 57. a) Write extended exercises, soprano and bas given. Make harmonic analysis.

    b) Bass only given. Write soprano line and fill in alto an tenor voices. Make harmonic analysis.

Other Part-Writing Considerations

a) The melodic augmented fourth. This interval is usually avoided in melodic writing, and therefore should not appear in any voice line in four-part writing. In the progression IV_6 - V, for example (see Figure 11.15*a*), the bass line may descend by the interval of diminished fifth (inversion of the augmented fourth), making possible a change of direction after the large leap. This necessary change of direction is impossible when using the augmented fourth, since the leading tone should resolve upwards.

b) Overlapping parts. Two adjacent parts (for example, tenor and bass) should not ascend to two tones above the higher of the two original tones, or descend to the reverse (see Figure 11.15*b*). Although examples of this procedure may be found in works of the best composers (the last phrases each of Bach chorales 47, 48 and 107), the procedure is comparatively infrequent and should be avoided when possible by the student at this time.

These overlapping parts may often be eliminated simply by changing the direction of one part, as in Figure 11.15*c* . In other cases, it will usually be necessary to change the position of the first of the two triads, or, if this is impossible, to change the position of a triad appearing before the pair in question.

Part-Writing Rule 7. Triad position may be changed
  a) at a repeated triad
  b) using Rule 2C
  c) at a triad in inversion or a triad with unusual doubling

In Figure 11.15*d*, changing the position of the second of the two V triads prevents the overlapping parts. In Figure 11.15*e*, it is necessary that the IV triad be in close position. This is possible only if the inner voices of the previous I₆ triad are changed.

Many part-writing difficulties other than the above can be solved by going back to a point where Rule 7 may be applied and rewriting the subsequent material.

Fig. 11.15.

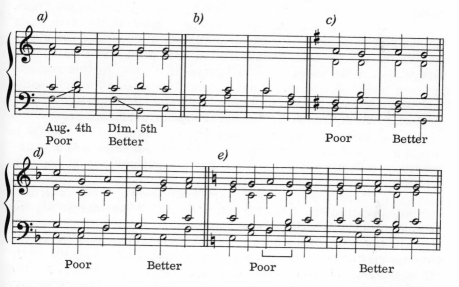

Assignment 58. Write on the staff the following progressions based on the given chord symbols. Other keys may be used.

a) D Major V_6 I

b) D♭ Major   I V_6 I

c) E Major IV_6 V I

d) G Minor V_6 i

e) B Minor iv_6 V i

f) F Minor   i IV_6 V_6 i

g) A Major   I IV I_6^4 V I

h) D♭ Major   ¾ I I_6 I │ V V_6 V │ I IV V │ I ‖

i) B Major   4/4 I │ IV_6 V_6 I I │ IV V I ‖

j) F♯ Minor   2/4 i V_6 │ i i_6 │ iv V │ i ‖

k) D Minor   4/4 V_6 │ i i iv V_6 │ i iv i_6^4 V │ I ‖

l) A♭ Major   ¾ V │ I IV V_6 │ I I_6 I │ IV_6 I_6^4 V │ I ‖

Performance of Part-Writing Exercises

Actual performance of part-writing exercises will allow the student to hear the musical effect of his efforts, particularly the effectiveness of the individual parts. Such performance may be accomplished in one of two ways.

As a choral performance. Copy out each of the four parts on separate pieces of paper for distribution to members of the class.

As an instrumental performance. Each of the four parts may be played on such orchestral or band instruments as are available in the theory class. Each of the four parts must be written separately for the use of individual players. Writing for instruments involves technical considerations ordinarily studied as instrumentation. Understanding of the following elementary principles of instrumentation will suffice in writing exercises for performance.

a) Range. Each instrument has one low note below which it cannot play, and an upper range above which its tones are unsatisfactory or difficult. Music written for an instrument must conform to this limitation.

b) Transposition. For some instruments, music is written with pitches differing from the actual sound. A clarinet in B♭, for example, sounds B♭ when the written pitch is C.

c) Clefs. Some instruments use clefs other than the treble and bass clef. The viola uses the alto clef almost exclusively, while other instruments use C clefs as needed.

Details concerning these three principles will be found as Appendix 2. Study these carefully before writing, and consult the player about the problems in playing his particular instrument.

Figure 11.16 illustrates the first few measures of the second exercise in Assignment 57, as written for clarinet in B♭, viola, horn in F and 'cello. Such a combination is not usual, but could occur in a classroom situation, and illustrates use of clefs and transposition.

Fig. 11.16.

AR TRAINING AND MUSIC READING

Exercise 73. Listening to triads in inversion. *a*) Identify the bass ote of a major triad as 1, 3, or 5 when the triad is played at the iano. Follow the same procedure used when identifying the soprano ote—sing the triad from the root, sing the bass note, and identify ne bass note by number.

b) Identify the bass note of a minor triad as 1, 3, or 5. Follow irections outlined in *a*) above.

c) Identify the bass note when major and minor triads are layed, as 1M, 5m, 5M, 3m, and so on.

d) Identify both soprano and bass note when major and/or ninor triads are played.

e) Spell the triad and the soprano note when the spelling of the ass note is given, or spell the triad and the bass note when the oprano note is given.

Exercise 74. Write the triad in inversion from dictation when the ass note is given. Procedure:

a) place given bass note on staff.

b) spell the triad after hearing it played.

c) write soprano note on staff.

d) fill in alto and tenor according to correct doubling pro- edures.

Exercise 75. Harmonic dictation. Listen to exercises containing riads in first and second inversion. Follow this procedure.

a) Write the chord numbers below the staff.

b) Write in soprano line on the treble staff.

c) Write in bass line on bass staff.

d) Indicate inversion in chord numbers (I_6, I_6, and so on). Check to see that note in bass line agrees.   4

Identifying the tonic six-four triad is sometimes troublesome. The bass note of the triad is the dominant tone of the key; this tone s held while the upper notes progress to a dominant triad. The ural effect of this dominant tone is that of a root of a triad above which are two non-harmonic tones (see Chapter 13) which resolve to he V triad. When the triad is tonic six-four, the dominant tone in he bass will be the fifth of the triad.

Self-Help in Harmonic Dictation

Students desiring to improve their ability in harmonic dictation can do so, working in pairs outside regular classroom instruction. One student will play the selected chord progression as the other vrites the chord numbers and the soprano and bass lines according o directions in Exercise 75. At this time, material can be derived rom two sources.

1. The part-writing exercises of this and preceding chapters make satisfactory harmonic dictation exercises. They may be played as written, or rewritten in other keys before playing (follow directions in Exercise 72). In addition, an exercise in a major key can be played in a minor key, or vice versa, by substituting an appropriate key signature.

2. Hymns provide excellent material for harmonic dictation exercises. Hymn books are universally procurable, and any hymn book will furnish examples illustrating most harmonic progressions. In this and following chapters, lists of excerpts from three representative hymnals will be given. These three are

The Hymnal of the Protestant Episcopal Church in the United States of America, hereinafter abbreviated *E.*

The Methodist Hymnal, abbreviated *M.*

The St. Gregory Hymnal and Catholic Choir Book, abbreviated *G*. The following information will be given.

a) The name of the hymn tune (see footnote, page 86) in *E* and *M*, and the title of the hymn in *G*. Many of the hymn tunes listed in *E* and *M* can be found in other Protestant hymnals by consulting the index of tunes. Harmonizations of the same tune in different hymnals occasionally vary.

b) The measure numbers to be used for harmonic dictation drill. In any hymn, measure 1 will be the *first complete* measure. The phrase for dictation may include one or more triads from the previous measure.

c) The number of the hymn (not the page number) in one of the three hymnals listed, for example, G-75 means hymn number 75 in the *St. Gregory Hymnal.*

Since these exercises are excerpts, it can be expected that many will begin and/or end on triads other than the tonic. In a very few cases, an occasional non-harmonic tone, a tone not belonging to the chord (circled in Figure 11.17), will be found on the weak part of a beat. These can be omitted in playing.

Example: Ellacombe 9-12 M-85. This means measures 9-12 of the hymn tune Ellacombe, to be found in the *Methodist Hymnal* as Number 85.

Fig. 11.17.

List of hymn tune examples containing I, IV and V triads only:

Praetorius 3-4	M-71	Webb 1-4	M-551
Adeste Fidelis 1-4	M-96		E-264
	E-12		
		Christe Sanctorum 1-4	E-157(2)
Invitation 1-4	M-190	Garden 1-4	E-202
Gethsemane 1-2	M-207	Ye Sons and Daughters 1-7	G-29
Louvan 9-12	M-307		
Eudoxia 1-4	M-308	Hail, Holy Queen 13-14	G-83
	E-172		
Henley 1-4	M-350		
More Love to Thee 1-2	M-364		
Tallis' Ordinal 1-2	M-478		
	E-298		

KEYBOARD HARMONY

Exercise 76. Play any major or minor triad in first or second inversion, with any member of the triad in the soprano. Use correct doubling.

Exercise 77. Play exercises from Assignments 55-57.

12

Rhythm:
Subdivision of the Beat

THEORY AND ANALYSIS

Musical examples studied thus far in rhythmic reading, rhythmic dictation and sight singing have utilized the divided beat only. By dividing equally each of the divided beats, subdivision of the beat results.

Fig. 12.1.

Exercise 78. Reading rhythmic patterns. While making a con-
luctor's beat and tapping the divided beat, read the following ex-
imples of subdivided beat. Read each line as many times as neces-
;ary before proceeding to the next line.

It is suggested that the syllable *ta* (*tah*) be used for all notes
;horter than the note value receiving one beat.

a) Simple time

Fig. 12.2.

Fig. 12.3.

Fig. 12.4.

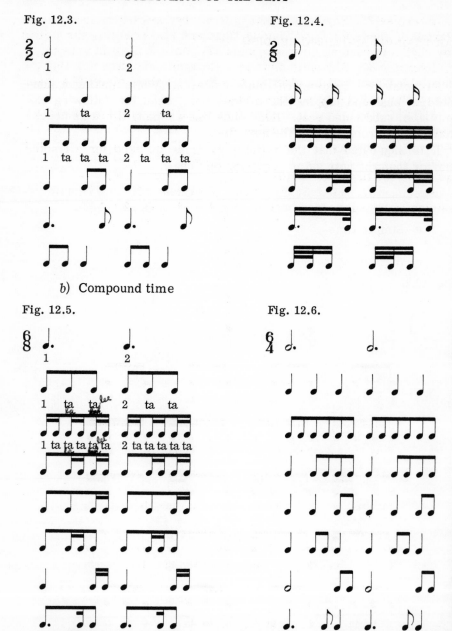

b) Compound time

Fig. 12.5.

Fig. 12.6.

Exercise 79. Rhythmic reading. Read rhythmically melodies from Part II of *Music for Sight Singing,* Chapters 11-14. Follow directions for rhythmic reading given on pages 37-38 of the present volume.

Exercise 80. Rhythmic dictation. Rhythmic dictation utilizing the subdivided beat will be given at this time.   Follow directions given for rhythmic dictation on pages 38-39.

Sight singing.   Sing melodies from Chapters 11-12 in *Music for Sight Singing.*   These contain the same melodic problems as already studied in Chapters 1-7 of that book.   The new problems   are rhythmic; all melodies in Part II of *Music for Sight Singing* illustrate the use of the subdivided beat.

Exercise 81.   Melodic dictation.   Exercises will now contain examples of the subdivided beat as found in Figures 12.1-12.5.

13

Non-Harmonic Tones (I)

THEORY AND ANALYSIS[1]

In the study of harmony and part-writing presented thus far, all notes in each of the four voice parts have been members of a triad. Actually, it is not common to find music in which all notes are parts of triads. There are usually other tones present which sound at the same time as the triad, but are not part of it. These are called *non-harmonic tones*. In Figure 13.1 the circled notes are the non-harmonic tones.

Fig. 13.1.   Bach, *Freuet euch, ihr Christen* (#8)

FA♭C   FA♭C   CE♭G   CE♭G   GBD   GBD   CEG

---

[1]Non-harmonic tones are presented at this time to enable the student to differentiate between harmonic and non-harmonic tones in a melodic line. With this knowledge, he can then learn to harmonize melodies at the keyboard, making practical use of his knowledge of the three principal triads. Further discussion of non-harmonic tones, including part-writing and exceptional practices, will be found in Chapter 19.

Music consisting entirely of pure harmony would become extremely dull to the ear. The addition of the dissonant effect of non-harmonic tones furnishes the necessary contrast to the purity of harmony to make the music more enjoyable. This can be illustrated by playing Figure 13.1, followed by a playing of the same example without its non-harmonic tones.

Fig. 13.2.

It will be observed that the non-harmonic tone is usually found melodically between two harmonic tones. At (1) in Figure 13.1 the non-harmonic tone G is found melodically between the two harmonic tones F and A♭, both harmonic tones belonging to the triad F A♭ C. At (2) the non-harmonic tone F appears between the harmonic tones G of the G B D triad and E of the C E G triad.

Definitions of Non-Harmonic Tones.[2]   Non-harmonic tones may be identified and classified by the relationship of the dissonance (the non-harmonic tone) to the harmonic tones which precede and follow it. To identify most non-harmonic tones, it is necessary to analyze the *three* notes involved—*a)* the harmonic tone preceding the dissonance, called the note of approach, *b)* the dissonance itself, and *c)* the harmonic tone following the dissonance, called the note of resolution.

There are several classifications into which non-harmonic tones may be placed.

a) Passing tone.   A non-harmonic tone which is found step-wise between harmonic tones of different pitch is known as a passing tone.

---

[2]There are in current use many names and conflicting definitions for the various non-harmonic tones. For comment on this problem, see "Terminology Variants" on page 133.

Fig. 13.3.

double passing tone

Occasionally, passing tones fill in the interval of a fourth between two harmonic tones, necessitating two passing tones adjacent to each other.

Fig. 13.4.

The second of the two passing tones above occurs on the beat, and is known as an accented passing tone, whereas the previous examples have been unaccented passing tones. Any non-harmonic tone occurring in a weak rhythmic position in relation to the note before and after it is designated as unaccented; any non-harmonic tone occurring in a strong rhythmic position in relation to the note before and after it is designated as an accented non-harmonic tone.

Fig. 13.5.

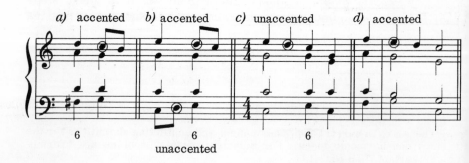

b) *Neighboring tone*. A non-harmonic tone which is found step-wise between two harmonic tones of the same pitch is known as a neighboring tone. When the dissonance is a step above the harmonic tone, it is called an upper neighboring tone; when it is below the harmonic tone, it is called a lower neighboring tone. Neighboring tones, although usually unaccented, may be found accented.

Fig. 13.6.

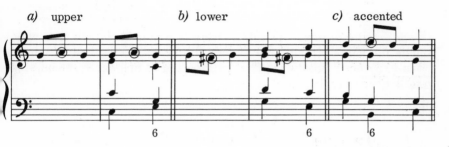

c) *Suspension*. A non-harmonic tone which is approached by a note of the same pitch and which resolves down by step or half-step is known as a suspension. The note of approach may be tied into the dissonance, as in Figure 13.7*c*, *d*, *e*, or not, as in Figure 13.7*b*.

Fig. 13.7.

the dissonance sounds here even though the note is not actually written at the point of dissonance

Less often, the dissonance in a suspension resolves upwards. This figure is sometimes known as a *retardation*.

Fig. 13.8.

d) *Anticipation*. An anticipation is a non-harmonic tone which sounds the same pitch as the harmonic tone following and is found in a weak rhythmic position. The anticipation is ordinarily found stepwise between two harmonic tones.

Fig. 13.9.

e) *Appoggiatura*. In the appoggiatura figure, the dissonance is approached by leap (interval of a third or larger) and resolves stepwise, usually in a direction opposite to the leap.

Fig. 13.10.

f) *Escaped tone* (also known as *Échappée*). In the escaped tone figure, the dissonance is approached by step and resolves by leap, usually in a direction opposite to that of the note of approach.

Fig. 13.11.

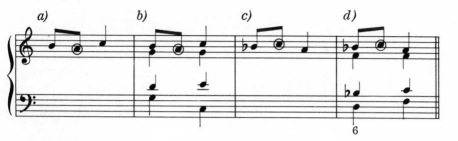

Examples of all of the preceding non-harmonic tones may be found in Figure 13.18, each identified by an abbreviation from Table 3. In addition, there are two non-harmonic tone figures in which more than three tones are involved.

g) Changing tone. This figure involves four notes. The note of approach and the note of resolution are the same pitch. The note of approach proceeds by step to a dissonance. This dissonant note skips an interval of a third in the opposite direction to a second dissonance, which in turn resolves step-wise to the note of resolution.

Fig. 13.12.

h) Pedal point (or Pedal; Organ point). The pedal point is a note sustained in one voice while in the other voices the harmonies are changing. It often occurs in the bass voice, whence the name pedal, referring to the practice of holding down one note with the foot on the pedal of the organ. When the sustained tone is found as the highest voice, it is known as an *inverted pedal*; when the sustained tone is found in an inner voice, it is known as an *inner pedal* or *internal pedal*.

TABLE 3

NON-HARMONIC TONES

Name of non-harmonic tone	Abbreviation	Example	Note of approach	Note of resolution	Direction of resolution
Passing tone, unaccented	UPT		Step-wise	Step-wise	Same direction as approach
Passing tone, accented	APT		Step-wise	Step-wise	Same direction as approach
Neighboring tone, upper	UN		Step-wise	Step-wise	Opposite to approach
Neighboring tone, lower	LN		Step-wise	Step-wise	Opposite to approach
Suspension	S		Same note	Step-wise	Down
Retardation	R		Same note	Step-wise	Up
Anticipation	A		Step-wise	Same note	Same note
Appoggiatura	App		By leap	Step-wise	Opposite to leap
Escaped tone	ET		Step-wise	By leap	Opposite to approach
Changing tones	CT		Step-wise	Step-wise	Same note as note of approach

Fig. 13.13.

I   V   I   V   I   IV   I

Terminology Variants

Terminologies for the various non-harmonic tones and the definitions of these terminologies vary widely and have never been standardized. Non-harmonic tones in general are also known as *non-chord tones, foreign tones, accessory tones* and *bytones*.

Non-harmonic tones are usually classified in one of two ways.

a) Each non-harmonic tone is named and defined according to the relationship of the dissonance to the harmonic tones which precede and follow it. Non-harmonic tones listed in the preceding pages of this chapter have been named and defined according to this principle.

b) Non-harmonic tones are grouped according to rhythmic placement:

(1) *accented non-harmonic tones*

(a) the *suspension,* in which the dissonance is tied over from its preceding note. The tied-over note of approach is called a *preparation*.

(b) the *appoggiatura,* a term which includes *all* other non-harmonic tones found in a strong rhythmic position. The term appoggiatura includes the following non-harmonic tones described in the preceding pages of this chapter: accented passing tone, accented neighboring tone, the suspension in which the note of approach is not tied into the dissonance, the appoggiatura occurring on an accented beat or part of beat, and the escaped tone occurring on an accented beat or part of beat.

(2) *unaccented non-harmonic tones*. These non-harmonic tones usually carry the same names as the unaccented non-harmonic tones described on pages 127-131. The neighboring tone, as defined on page 129, is sometimes known as a *changing tone* or an *auxiliary tone*.

The name appoggiatura is also given to a small note appearing before a principal note in a melody. This appoggiatura receives half of the value of the note following, unless the note following is a dotted note, in which case the appoggiatura receives two thirds of the value of the following note.

Fig. 13.14.   Excerpts from Haydn, *The Creation*

This appoggiatura is not to be confused with the *grace note,* a note which looks like an appoggiatura but with a slash across the stem (♪). The grace note is performed without specific time value and as quickly as possible.

Fig. 13.15.   Haydn, *The Creation*

The above is not a complete survey of the appoggiatura. The no- tation and the use of the appoggiatura, as well as the other non- harmonic tones, is often directly related to the historical period in which the device is used. For complete information, the student is referred to articles on non-harmonic tones in standard musical reference works, such as *Grove's Dictionary of Music and Musicians* and the *Harvard Dictionary of Music* by Willi Apel.

Analysis of Non-Harmonic Tones

a) In chorales. The chorales of Johann Sebastian Bach offer unlimited opportunity for study of non-harmonic tones. Each of the four melodic lines in any chorale displays many of them. To identify these non-harmonic tones, it is necessary first to spell the chord; those notes not belonging to the chord will be non-harmonic tones which can be positively identified by relating the dissonant note to its preceding and following notes.

The examples for analysis may contain chords not yet studied. In such cases, merely arrange the notes in a series of thirds to spell the triad or chord; any remaining notes will be non-harmonic.

Fig. 13.16.   Bach, *Wer nur den lieben Gott* (#146)

ACE   ACE   EG#B ACE G#BD ACE BDF EG#B   EG#B

Note that when an accented non-harmonic tone is used, the chord tone is the note following the accented non-harmonic tone, as in the third chord (E G# B) above.

The identification of the note located at the interval of a seventh above the root is sometimes difficult because it often seems to be a chord tone (seventh of a chord) and a non-harmonic tone at the same time. For the present, consider such tones as chord tones when they are accented, and as non-harmonic when they are unaccented. Further discussion and clarification of this problem will be found in Chapters 19 and 20.

Fig. 13.17.   Bach, *O Ewigkeit, du Donnerwort* (#26)

GB♭DF CEG(B♭)

Assignment 58. Identify non-harmonic tones circled, but not already labeled, in Figure 13.18. Use abbreviations as given in table of non-harmonic tones, page 132.

Assignment 58.

Fig. 13.18.   Bach, *Jesu, Jesu, du bist mein* (#244)

* ⊗ = note held over sounds non-harmonic at this point

Assignment 59. Copy out phrases from Bach chorales listed below. Circle the non-harmonic tones and identify each.

No.			
2 first phrase		167 first, second and third phrases
5 last phrase		201 first phrase
22 first phrase		219 first phrase
49 first phrase		349 first phrase
111 first phrase		

b) In instrumental music. Music written for instruments may be analyzed by the principles given for chorales. In keyboard music, chords are often found "broken," that is, single notes of the chord are played in succession, extending, usually, through one or more beats. In such cases, it is only necessary to reassemble the chord, as in Figure 13.19.

Fig. 13.19.   Mozart, Sonata for Piano in C Major, K. 279, first movement

Non-harmonic tones are often chromatically altered—they may be found with an accidental not belonging to the key, as the appoggiatura C♯ in Figure 13.19. Such chromatic alterations do not affect the analysis. Occasionally, two non-harmonic tones will be found in succession, without an intervening harmonic tone.

Assignment 60.[3] From the music scores listed below, copy out the measures indicated. Below the bass line write in chord spellings

[3]Assignments in harmonic analysis in this text will be found in one or more of these sources—Bach, *371 Chorales*, Beethoven, Sonatas for Piano (numbers 1-12 only), Chopin, Mazurkas, Mendelssohn, *Songs Without Words,* Mozart, Sonatas for Piano, and Schumann, *Album for the Young,* Op. 68.

Examples from Murphy and Melcher, *Music for Study* (Englewood Cliffs, N.J.: Prentice-Hall, Inc., 1960) may be used in place of the sources listed. Appropriate chapter numbers from *Music for Study,* will be listed in each assignment in harmonic analysis.

and the chord numbers (only I, IV, V and V^7 chords will be found). Circle all non-harmonic tones and identify each with proper abbreviation. These steps are shown in Figure 13.19.

Measure 1 in any composition is the *first complete* measure. Repeats indicated by repeat signs are not numbered. First endings are not numbered. Do not analyze grace notes.

Beethoven, Sonata for Piano No. 5 (Op. 10, No. 1), second movement, measures 1-9.
Chopin, Mazurka No. 16 (Op. 24, No. 3), measures 1-12.
Mendelssohn, *Songs Without Words*
    No. 12 (Op. 30, No. 6), measures 15-21
    No. 37 (Op. 85, No. 1), measures 1-5
Mozart, Sonatas for Piano
    G Major, K. 283, first movement, measures 1-10
    A Major, K. 331, third movement, last 31 measures
Schumann, *Album for the Young,* Op. 68
    No. 8, measures 1-8, 9-16   No. 11, measures 25-28
                    No. 19, measures 1-4
Murphy and Melcher, *Music for Study*: Chapter 1 (I triad), Chapter 2 (V and V^7, root in bass), Chapter 3 (IV triad), Chapter 4 (Tonic Six-four), Chapter 5 (I, IV and V in first inversion), and Chapter 7 (V^7 in inversion).

Determinants of the Harmonic Background of a Melodic Line

In studying the harmonization of a melodic line, we have considered that each note of the melody would bear its own triad. Harmonizing a melody with a chord for each note is common practice in church hymns, but quite uncommon elsewhere, such as in a folk song, an art song, a melody in a symphony, a clarinet solo, and so on. Occasionally a melody other than a hymn tune may be found in which no non-harmonic tones are implied, such as melody number 18 from Part I of *Music for Sight Singing*. Most often, however, the melodic line contains tones implying both harmonic and non-harmonic usages.

Fig. 13.20.   German Folk Song (MSS I-24)

In creating a harmonization for a given melody, it is necessary
to know which melody tones are harmonic or non-harmonic.   In
addition, three other factors—*a)* chord succession, *b)* tempo, and
c) harmonic rhythm—will play an important part in the choice of
chords and also in the ultimate determination of which melodic tones
are harmonic and which non-harmonic.

a) Chord succession. Most folk tunes and the more simple
composed melodies can be harmonized using I, IV and V only. These
same tunes can be harmonized with more complex harmonies, as
will be done later, but for the present only three principal triads
will be used.

Making use of the three principal triads, the following progressions are possible.

I - V	IV - I	V - I
I - IV	IV - V	V - IV *retrograde*

The V - IV is infrequently found in music and should therefore be
used sparingly by the student at this time.   For an example of an
appropriate use of the V - IV progression, see melody number 163,
measures 4-5, from Part I of *Music for Sight Singing*.

Occasionally the fourth scale step in the melodic line will imply
the seventh of a V^7 chord. In this case, it is only necessary to add a
V triad to make a complete V^7 chord.

Fig. 13.21.   German Folk Song (MSS I-28)

implied harmony:

A IV triad harmonization would be possible in the third full measure of the example above. Since both IV and V^7 are technically correct, the choice will be dictated by the individual student's musica
taste.

Care should be taken that each phrase end with some form o
cadence, authentic or plagal. In the following example, the end of the
phrase could be harmonized with successive I triads, but this is un-
musical because of the lack of a cadence.

Fig. 13.22.   French Folk Song (MSS I-75)

b) *Tempo*. As a rule of thumb, it can be said that ordinarily a
new chord or a repetition of a previous chord will be placed at each
principal beat in the measure, for example, two chords per measure
in $\frac{2}{4}$ time, three chords per measure in $\frac{3}{4}$ time, two chords per
measure in $\frac{6}{8}$ time, and so on. In very slow tempi, more chords per
measure may be needed, while in very fast tempi, the call is for
fewer chords per measure. In Figure 13.23, the melody to be harmonized has been given three different tempi markings to illustrate
the effect on chord selection. If this melody were marked *very slow*
as in *a*), then the tempo is felt as six beats per measure, indicating
the desirability of changing the chord on each of those beats where a
change of melody note occurs. In the more common moderate tempo
b), the chord changes are more likely to occur on the strong beats
of the measure, in this case two beats per measure. When the tempo
is rapid, one chord per measure often suffices, as in *c*).

Fig. 13.23.   French Folk Song (MSS I-47)

a) Very slow

It cannot be specifically stated how slow or fast the tempo must
be before determining how often a chord change is desirable. This
can be determined only by careful study of the melody and applying
one's own aesthetic judgment.

c) Harmonic rhythm. The rhythmic pattern established by the
frequency of chord change is known as harmonic rhythm. In a piece
of music, the harmony may change on each beat of the bar.

Fig. 13.24.[4]   Bach, *Du Friedensfürst, Herr Jesu Christ* (#42)

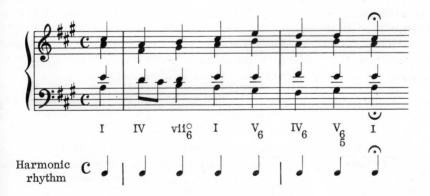

It is also possible that the music may cover several measures with
no change of harmony at all.

---

[4]V_6^5 = V^7 in first inversion. See Chapter 20.

Fig. 13.25.   Beethoven, Symphony No. 3, first movement

These are extremes in the application of harmonic rhythm. More commonly found are harmonic rhythm patterns in which there are durations of unequal length.

Fig. 13.26.   Foster, *Old Folks at Home*

The question arises as to when, rhythmically, a chord change should be made. In general, the strong beats of the harmonic rhythm should coincide with the strong beats of the meter. This statement implies the following observations.

   1) Chords may be changed on any beat of the measure.

   2) When a new chord (a chord different from the preceding chord) appears on a strong beat of the measure, it may extend into following beats.

   3) When a new chord appears on a weak beat of the measure, it should not be repeated on a following stronger beat. A new chord should appear on the following stronger beat. This also holds true for a bass note; a bass note appearing on a weak beat should not be

epeated on the following strong beat, even if there is a change in harmony.

4) Exceptions

The chord appearing on the opening weak beat of a piece of music or of a new phrase may be repeated on the following strong beat. Often, however, no harmony at all is supplied at such points.

Fig. 13.27.   Schubert, *Klage an den Mond* (MSS II-43)

A new phrase beginning on a strong beat may repeat the harmony of the previous weak beat.

Fig. 13.28.   Spanish Folk Song (MSS I-86)

The above observations concerning harmonic rhythm will cover most situations, but occasional places in tunes may be encountered in which it will be necessary to violate these "rules."

The following melody is harmonized two different ways to show the effect of incorrect and correct application of the principles of harmonic rhythm. The chord succession in both harmonizations is good. However, beginning in the second measure of the first harmonization *a)* the chord newly appearing on the second (weak) beat is consistently repeated on the following strong beat, giving an awkward effect of displacement of the natural accent of the melody.

Fig. 13.29.   French Folk Song (MSS II-18)

Examples in which it is possible to interpret the melody in two wide
ly different ways are not common.   Most melodies are more likely
to follow the example of Figure 13.23*b* where the nature of th
melody demands a chord choice in which the harmonic rhythm i,
correct.

Assignment 61. Melodic Analysis.   Copy out melodies as as
signed from Chapters 1-7 and 11-12 in *Music for Sight Singing*. O
a bass staff below the melody, write in the implied harmony in bloc
triads with the correct triad number.   Circle non-harmonic tones i
the melody and identify each by name (abbreviation).   Use Figur
13.20 as a guide.

It is suggested that some of the following numbers from *Musi*
for Sight Singing be used as the first problems in this assignment
as well as for Exercise 82.

Melodies requiring I and V triads only: 3, 9, 10, 11, 13, 14, 19
28.

Melodies in which the location of the IV triad is easily discerni
ble: Part I - 99, 142, 163; Part II - 28, 31.

Others: Part I - 31, 33, 40, 44, 46, 78, 92, 93.

APPLICATION

KEYBOARD HARMONY

Melodies and their harmonizations from Assignment 61 may b
played at the keyboard as written with block triads in root positio
in the left hand against the melody in the right hand.   Such a pro
cedure will serve as an introduction to keyboard harmonization
however, the use of such block triads on the piano often produces
thick ugly sound when played in a low register and, of course, alway
produces parallel fifths.   For a more musical effect, the triads o
the implied harmony may be played in any one of several othe
styles, three of which are shown in Figure 13.30.

ig. 13.30.

German Folk Song (MSS I - 28)

a) close position in right hand

I   I   V   I

b) open position, both hands

c) rhythmic accompaniment in left hand

he left hand accompaniment in Figure 13.30 *c* can be adapted to any
eter scheme.

d)

or   etc.

It will often be useful to harmonize a cadence with the I_6,
4

specially with a soprano line of 3-2-1 or 1-7-1. It can be preceded
I or IV, but should not be preceded by V. The tonic six-four must
pear on a strong beat of the measure (or may appear on the sec-
d beat in $\frac{3}{4}$ time), followed by the V triad.

g. 13.31.

English Folk Song (MSS I-41)

a)

i   i$_6$ V   i
                       4

German Folk Song (MSS II-23)

Students working in pairs can practice keyboard harmonization and sight singing simultaneously. While one student sings the melody (or plays it on an instrument), the other will accompany him. In this procedure, the melody need not be played by the keyboard player; instead, he may divide the accompaniment figure between the two hands. A few such methods of accompaniment are shown in Figure 13.32.

Fig. 13.32.   English Folk Song (MSS I-6)

Exercise 82. Play melodies with accompaniment of tonic, dominant and sub-dominant triads at the keyboard, using piano accompaniment styles shown in Figures 13.30 and 13.32. Melodies may be played from Chapters 1-7 and 11-12 in *Music for Sight Singing*.

14

The Leading
Tone Triad

THEORY AND ANALYSIS

The Secondary Triads

The secondary triads in a key are those built on scale steps other than I, IV and V. In a major key, these triads are[1]

Fig. 14.1.

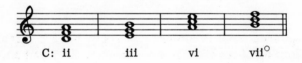

C: ii   iii   vi   vii°

In a minor key, alternate forms of the triads appear because of the use of different forms of the minor scale.

Fig. 14.2

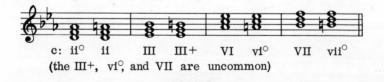

c: ii° ii   III III+   VI vi°   VII vii°
(the III+, vi°, and VII are uncommon)

---

[1]For meaning of chord numbering symbols, review Chapter 2.

The Diminished Triad

The diminished triad is composed of two minor thirds. The resulting distance between the root and the fifth of the diminished triad is the interval of a diminished fifth (one half step smaller than a perfect fifth); the interval of the diminished fifth when inverted becomes an augmented fourth.

Fig. 14.3.

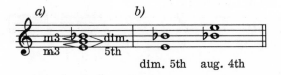

dim. 5th   aug. 4th

Because of the interval of the diminished fifth, the diminished triad is classified as one of the dissonant triads.[2] Both the interval of the diminished fifth and its inversion, the augmented fourth, are known commonly as a *tritone,* referring to the fact that the interval is composed of three whole steps (six half steps). The interval equally divides the octave.

Fig. 14.4.

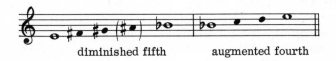

diminished fifth   augmented fourth

The diminished triad is almost invariably used in first inversion. Typical examples of its use are seen in Figs. 14.5 and 14.6.

Fig. 14.5.   Bach, *Nun ruhen alle Wälder* (#117)

---

[2]Consonant triads are defined (in the historical period under study) as those containing consonant intervals: the octave, perfect fifth, perfect fourth, major and minor thirds, major and minor sixths. Triads or chords containing other intervals are dissonant.

Fig. 14.6.   Mozart, Sonata in D Major for Piano, K. 284,
                                                            third movement

Assignment 62. Spell diminished triads,
    a) when each of the following is the root of the triad (example:
G—G B♭ D♭): A, C♯, B, E, B♭, A♭, C, E♯, A♯, F✗;
    b) when each of the following is the third of the triad (exam-
ple: G—E G B♭): F, B♭, C♯, D, F♯, G♯, C, F♭, B, D♯;
    c) when each of the following is the fifth of the triad (example:
G—C♯ E G): C, A, F, A♭, F♯, D♭, C♯, C♭, D♯, B.

The Triad on the Leading Tone

The triad on the leading tone is a diminished triad in both major
and minor keys. The symbol is vii°. The triad is most often found in
first inversion (vii°₆), as in Figure 14.5.
    Assignment 63. Spell the vii° triad in each major and minor key.

The vii° triad is often used as a substitute for the V triad, at the
cadence and within the phrase, most commonly in these two situations.[3]
    a) Between the tonic triad and its first inversion (Figure 14.7)
or reverse (Figure 14.9).

---

[3]The diminished triad sonority (vii° or ii°) caused by the passing tone
will be discussed in Chapter 15.

Fig. 14.7.   Bach, *Ach Gott, vom Himmel sieh' darein* (#3)

V   i   vii°₆   i₆   V₄₃   i   V₆   i   V

Rule 6A

b) After the IV triad when the melody ascends by step.

Fig. 14.8.   Carol: *Good King Wenceslas*

IV   I₆   IV   vii°₆   I   I

The leading tone triad is usually preceded by the tonic triad (as in Figure 14.7) or by the subdominant triad (as in Figure 14.8). Rarely does the V triad either precede or follow the vii° triad.

Assignment 64. Harmonic analysis. In each of the following phrases from Bach chorales, find the vii°₆ triad and describe its use. Phrases marked * contain only triads studied thus far; make complete analysis of triads and non-harmonic tones.

*26, first phrase	*267, first phrase
*47, first phrase	273, fourth phrase
*178, first phrase	289, first phrase
*244, first phrase	363, first phrase

See also Murphy and Melcher, *Music for Study,* Chapter 13. (These contain triads not yet studied.)

Terminology Variant

The vii°₆ triad is often identified by the symbol V°⁷, meaning an incomplete V⁷ chord. B D F is an incomplete G B D F chord.

APPLICATION

WRITTEN MATERIALS

Writing the Diminished Triad

Use of any diminished triad in other than first inversion is so un-common that only first inversion will be considered at this time.

The normal voice distribution for any diminished triad in first inversion is two thirds, one root and one fifth (bass note doubled). However, when the triad is found with the fifth in the soprano, the fifth is usually doubled (two fifths, one root, one third).

Fig. 14.9.   Bach, *Zeuch uns nach Dir*

Fig. 14.10.   Bach, *Aus meines Herzens Grunde* (#1

Assignment 65. Writing diminished triads. Double the third when the root or third is in the soprano; double the fifth when the fifth is in the soprano.

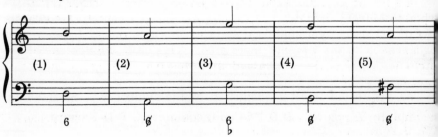

Writing the Leading Tone Triad

a) *Use of Rule 6A.* Since this triad is used almost exclusively in first inversion, part-writing Rule 6A may be used in approaching and leaving the triad. See progression i vii$^o_6$ i$_6$ in Figure 14.7.

b) *IV - vii$^o_6$.* Use of the vii$^o_6$ instead of V following the IV triad when the melody ascends (as in Figures 14.5 and 14.8) is necessary to prevent parallel fifths and octaves. Should the progression IV-V be used with an ascending melody line, it would be impossible to follow part-writing Rule 3 (triads with roots in the bass a second apart).[4]

Fig. 14.11.

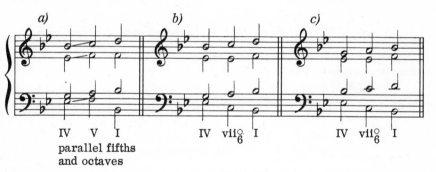

In a minor key, the subdominant triad is often a major triad (IV) when the melody ascends. The progression IV-vii$^o_6$ will include, as one of the voice parts, the melodic line in which the sixth scale step progresses to the seventh scale step. This calls for the use of the melodic minor scale, the raised sixth in turn causing the subdominant triad to become major.

---

[4] For an example of such a IV-V progression, see Bach chorale number 77, first phrase. This procedure is little used.

Fig. 14.12.

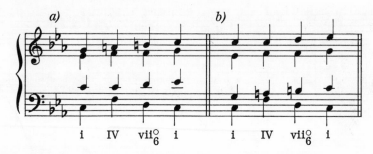

c) *Unequal fifths.* There sometimes appear in the progression I-vii° or vii°-I pairs of fifths which seem to be parallel. If the part-writing is correct, the fifths will be *unequal fifths*, that is, one is a perfect fifth, the other a diminished fifth.

Fig. 14.13.

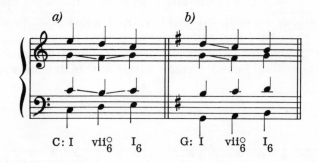

See examples in Figures 14.10 and 14.14.

d) *vii⁰₆ with the fifth in the soprano.* As a melody tone, the fifth of the vii⁰₆ triad (or any diminished triad) normally descends, as in Figure 14.10. It may progress upwards when found in a melody line moving in similar motion with the bass at the interval of a tenth (an octave plus a third).

Fig. 14.14.   Bach, *Vater unser im Himmelreich* (#47)

Assignment 66. Part-writing. Fill in alto and tenor voices. Be
particularly careful of the approach and resolution of all doubled
notes in triads in first inversion. As usual, write in triad numbers
below the bass part.

Assignment 67. Part-writing, bass line only given. Supply
melody line and fill in alto and tenor parts.

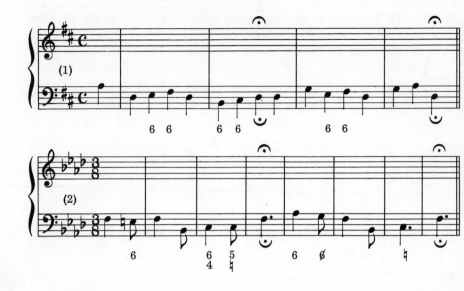

Assignment 68. Write in four voices the following progressions.

a) D Major $\frac{3}{4}$ V | I$_6$ vii$^o_6$ I | IV$_6$ I$_6\atop4$ V | I ‖

b) G^b Major $\frac{4}{4}$ I | IV vii$^o_6$ I I$_6$ | IV V I ‖

c) G minor $\frac{2}{4}$ V | i i$_6$ | vii$^o_6$ i | iv V | i ‖

d) B^b minor $\frac{4}{4}$ V | i i IV* vii$^o_6$ | i iv i$_6\atop4$ V | i ‖

*Third or fifth of triad in soprano.

Melody Harmonization

The Triad in Inversion. In harmonizing melodies from previous chapters, we have always placed the root of the triad in the bass. The result has usually been a series of large skips in the bass voice. Though it is more acceptable to have such skips in the bass than in the other voices, it is preferable that the bass line be made more melodic, either by reducing the number of large leaps or the size of these leaps. This can be accomplished by the use of triads in inversion. Compare the bass lines of the two examples below, the first of which is a Bach chorale and the second the same harmonization with the root of each chord in the bass part.

Fig. 14.15.   Bach, *Was Gott tut, das ist wohlgetan* (#293)

The triad to be used for each melody note should be chosen first when harmonizing a melody. With the use of inversions, it now becomes necessary to decide which triads will be in inversion and which will have the root in the bass, so the bass line should be written *before* the alto and tenor. The soprano and bass together should make a good two-part composition.

When the bass line moves with the soprano, their related movements can be in any one of four directions.

a) *contrary motion* to each other

b) *oblique motion*—soprano stays on same tone while bass moves, or soprano moves while bass maintains the same tone

c) *similar motion* to each other

d) *stationary motion*—both soprano and bass repeat their tones.

Fig. 14.16.

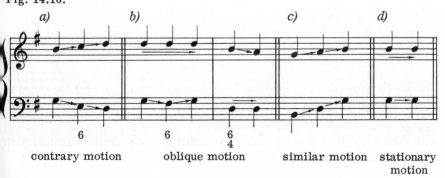

contrary motion   oblique motion   similar motion   stationary
                                                              motion

By extracting the soprano and bass only from Figure 14.15 we can find the following types of motion.

Fig. 14.17.

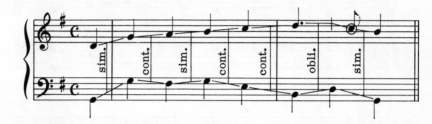

Of the four types of motion, contrary and oblique are the most frequently used, although similar motion is good when found as intervals of thirds or sixths between soprano and bass.[5] (See Figures 14.15 and 14.17, progression from 3rd to 4th chord.) Inversions should be chosen to make the bass line progress more by intervals of seconds and thirds rather than by larger leaps. Note, however, that cadences are usually more effective when their triads have roots in the bass. For the present, the first inversion only will be used, except that the I_4^6 may be used at a cadence.

---

[5]At this point, consideration should be given to the "hidden octave" and the "hidden fifth" (sometimes called "direct octave" and "direct fifth"). A hidden octave occurs when two voices progress in similar motion to a perfect octave; a hidden fifth occurs when two voices progress in similar motion to a perfect fifth.

hidden 8ves   hidden 5ths

These need concern the student *only* when they occur between the two outer voices of a composition. Even then they are acceptable when *a)* the chord is repeated (Figure 14.17, first two chords) or *b)* when the triad roots are a fifth apart (Figure 14.9, progression I-V at the fermata). In other circumstances hidden octaves and fifths between outer voices often do not sound well. Any such octave or fifth should be used only after careful consideration of its aural effect.

By following the above directions, several possible bass lines can be found to fit a given melody, final choice to be dictated by musical taste. The following examples show how each of two melodies could be harmonized in a number of different ways.

Fig. 14.18.   Fig. 14.19.

Chord Progression Review.[6] Commonly used progressions using the I, IV, V and vii° triads studied thus far (symbols apply to major and minor keys) are listed on the following page.

_____

[6]Chord progressions listed here (similar lists will be found in Chapters 15 and 17) are those which have been described as commonly used progressions. The student would do well at this time to limit his choice of chords to these. Any chord progression not listed can be found in actual music; discussion and study of these less frequently used progressions will be found in Ottman, *Advanced Harmony: Theory and Practice,* (Englewood Cliffs, N.J.: Prentice-Hall, Inc., 1961), Chapter 3.

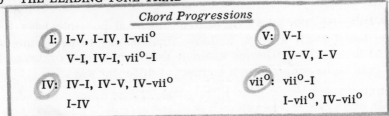

Assignment 69. Melody harmonization. Supply harmony and three lower voice parts when melody only is given. As this is a problem in diminished triads, use the vii°₆ triad wherever practicable.

Assignment 70. Write original exercises using the four triads studied to date. Write four-measure phrases or periods, as assigned. Write for voices or instruments, as assigned. Pay particular attention to *a)* chord choice, *b)* harmonic rhythm, *c)* melodic writing and *d)* the bass line. In addition, indicate the tempo of your composition and include dynamic markings.

The Diminished Triad

Exercise 83. Singing diminished triads. From a given pitch, sing a diminished triad, calling the given pitch 1, 3 or 5, as directed, or sing with pitch names when the name of the given pitch is supplied.

ig. 14.20.

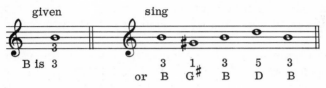

Exercise 84. Identifying the soprano when the diminished triad is played. For this ear training exercise, the diminished triad will be played in first inversion only. Follow this procedure.

    a) Listen to triad.

    b) Sing triad from root, bearing in mind that the bass tone heard is always "3."

    c) Sing the soprano note.

    d) Identify the soprano note as 1, 3 or 5.

    e) Spell the triad when the name of the soprano note is given.

Exercise 85. Identifying the tritone by ear. Since both the diminished fifth and the augmented fourth are exactly the same size, t is impossible to differentiate between them unless a chord is sounded at the same time.

ig. 14.21.

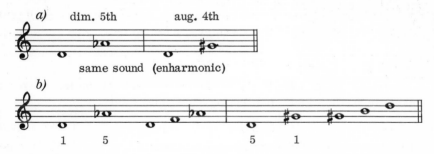

Procedure

    a) Listen to interval, followed by playing of triad.

    b) Sing triad from root, singing 1-3-5-3-1.

    c) Sing interval with correct numbers.

    d) Identify interval as diminished fifth (1 up to 5 or 5 down to
.) or as an augmented fourth (5 up to 1 or 1 down to 5).

Fig. 14.22.

Spell the interval or write interval on the staff when the name of the first note is given.

The Leading Tone Triad

Exercise 86. *a)* Singing the leading tone triad. In the given key (major or minor) sing the progression I-vii°-I or i-vii°-i. Sing each triad from its root with letter names.

b) Sing the progression I IV vii° I or i IV vii° i in the given key.

Exercise 87. Harmonic dictation. The vii° can easily be identified, as it is a diminished triad and generally progresses directly to the tonic triad. Any or all of the following steps will be helpful in distinguishing the various triads studied thus far.

a) After listening to dictation exercise, write down the *type* of each triad, using the symbol *M* for major, *m* for minor and *d* for diminished.

b) Sing with scale numbers or with letter names as directed the root of each triad as the progression is played.

c) Sing each triad with the numbers 1-3-5, or sing each triad with correct spelling in the given key, as directed.

Self-Help in Harmonic Dictation

Excerpts from hymns listed below contain examples of tonic subdominant, dominant and leading tone triads only.

Ratisbon	1-2	M-32, E-153	Alida	1-4	M-522
Olivet	7-10	M-176	Petra	9-10	E-70
Gräfenberg	7-9	M-389	Doncaster	1-4	E-293
Schumann	1-2	M-456	Spanish Chant	5-6	E-332
		Silver Street	11-12	E-552	

Upon completion of Assignment 70, each of two students working together may use his original composition as a harmonic dictation exercise by playing his composition while the other student takes down the triad numbers and the soprano and bass lines. This procedure should be continued in each subsequent chapter.

KEYBOARD HARMONY

Exercise 88. Play cadences in Figure 14.23 in any major or minor key.

Fig. 14.23.

Exercise 89. Play examples from Assignments 66 and 68 at the keyboard.

15

The Supertonic Triad

THEORY AND ANALYSIS

In a major key, the supertonic triad is a minor triad (ii). In a minor key it is a diminished triad (ii°) or a minor triad (ii) when used in conjunction with the melodic minor scale.

Fig. 15.1.

C: ii   c: ii°   ii

Assignment 71. Spelling the supertonic triad.
   a) Spell the ii triad in each major key.
   b) Spell the ii° triad in each minor key.
   c) Spell the ii triad in each minor key.

The supertonic triad is most commonly used in first inversion in both major and minor keys. In a minor key the ii° triad, being diminished, is always in first inversion.

The supertonic triad is ordinarily followed by V, vii°$_6$ or, when in first inversion, may also be followed by tonic six-four chord at the cadence. Of the triads studied thus far it may be preceded by the tonic triad and the subdominant triad. Typical examples of the use of the supertonic triad follow.

Fig. 15.2 ii–V

Hymn: Hanover

Fig. 15.3.[1] (ii)–vii$^o_6$

Bach, *O Welt, sieh hier dein Leben* (#363)

The spelling B D F$\sharp$, ii in A major (third chord in Figure 15.3) is caused by the presence of the accented passing tone in the G$\sharp$ B D triad. Were this passage found in a very slow tempo, the B D F$\sharp$ sonority could be analyzed as a ii triad.

Fig. 15.4. ii$_6$–V

Haydn, Sonata in D Major for Piano, first movement

---

[1]V$_4\atop2$ = V[7] in third inversion. See Chapter 20.

Fig. 15.5. ii$^0_6$-V

Bach, *Wo soll ich fliehen hin* (#281)

i   ii$_6$ V

Fig. 15.6. ii$_6$-I$_6^4$

Hymn: Petra

I   ii$_6$ I$_6^4$ V   I

Assignment 72. Harmonic analysis. The following excerpts contain examples of the supertonic triad and triads previously studied. Spell each chord, identify it by number and inversion, and identify non-harmonic tones.

Beethoven: Sonata for Piano, No. 1 (Op. 2, No. 1), fourth movement, measures 59-68.
Chopin: Mazurka No. 23 (Op. 33, No. 2), measures 1-8.
Mendelssohn: *Songs Without Words*
    No. 8 (Op. 30, No. 2), measures 5-8
    No. 39 (Op. 85, No. 3), measures 1-3
Mozart: Sonatas for Piano
    G Major, K. 283, first movement, measures 36-38 (in D major)
    C Major, K. 279, first movement, measures 1-4, 31-33 (in G major)
    D Major, K. 284, third movement, variation 7, measures 1-3
Schumann: *Album for the Young,* Op. 68
    No. 20, last 8 measures
    No. 22, measures 1-4
Murphy and Melcher, *Music for Study*, Chapter 6

APPLICATION

WRITTEN MATERIALS

Alternate doubling in minor triads. In addition to the normal doublings already studied, a minor triad is commonly found with the third of the triad doubled (regardless of soprano note), particularly when this third is one of the three primary scale tones of the key—tonic, subdominant and dominant. In the case of the ii triad, the third of the triad is the subdominant tone of the key, so it is commonly doubled.

Fig. 15.7.   Fig. 15.8.   Hymn: Orientis Partibus

See also Figure 15.13.

Writing the supertonic triad. Most progressions in which the supertonic triad is found can be written with part-writing rules already presented.

Rule 2A or 2B: ii - V. See Figures 15.9 *a* and *b*, and 15.2.

Rule 3:   I(i) - ii. (not common).

Rule 6A: Any progression in which the ii or ii^{O} triad is in first inversion. See Figure 15.9 *c* and *d*. Also Figures 15.5, 15.6 and 15.8.

Fig. 15.9.

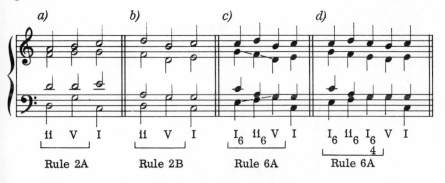

The following progressions require new procedures.

a) (ii)-vii$^{o}_{6}$. This progression has been described in conjunction with Figure 15.3. The figured bass is "5 6." See Figures 15.10, 15.11 and 15.13.

Fig. 15.10.

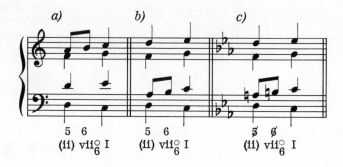

Fig. 15.11.   Bach, *Wo soll ich fliehen hin* (#25)

b) I - ii with ascending melody line (in major). In this progression, the roots of the two triads are in the bass and are a second apart, but since the melody progresses in the same direction as the bass, Rule 3 cannot be used.

Part-Writing Rule 5.   When it is impossible to follow normal rules for triads with roots in bass, double the third in the second of the two triads.

Progression to and from the doubled third is handled by use of Rule 6A.

Fig. 15.12.

Fig. 15.13.   Hymn: St. Thomas

Rule 5

c) IV - ii. The part-writing procedures (Rule 4A, 4B) for this progression will be presented in Chapter 16 in conjunction with more widely used progressions. See Figure 15.2 for an example of IV - ii.

Assignment 73. Writing the supertonic triad. Fill in alto and tenor voices. Make harmonic analysis.

Assignment 74. Fill in soprano, alto, and tenor voices when bass line only is given. Make harmonic analysis.

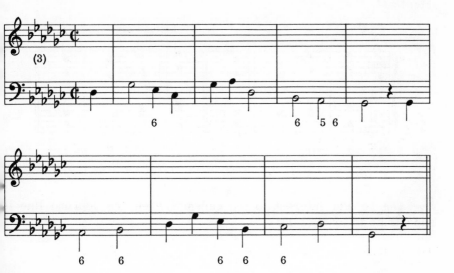

Assignment 75. Write the following harmonic progressions in our parts. Choose a time signature and write a progression that is rhythmically interesting and displays acceptable harmonic rhythm.

✓ *a)* E♭ Major   I ii$_6$ I$_6$ vii$^o_6$ I IV V I

b) F minor   V i i$_6$ vii$^o_6$ i ii$^o_6$ V i

c) B Major   V I$_6$ V$_6$ I I ii$_6$ V I I IV vii$^o_6$ I ii$_6$ I$_6$ V I

                                                                        4

In the following progressions, no inversions are indicated. Choose inversions which will make a good bass line.

✓ *d)* A Major   I I IV vii^o I vii^o I ii I V I

e) F minor   i iv V i vii^o i i V V i ii^o i V I

f) D♭ Major   V V I IV vii^o I ii vii^o I ii I V I

Melody Harmonization Using the Supertonic Triad

The supertonic triad can often be used in place of either the dominant or subdominant triads in harmonizing a melody. Several possibilities follow.

a) To add variety to harmony, avoiding repetition of a triad.

Fig. 15.14.

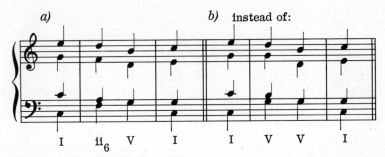

To add interest to the cadence when the soprano line is supertonic to tonic (2-1).

b)

Fig. 15.15.

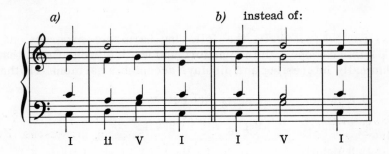

c) As a substitute for the subdominant triad.

Fig. 15.16.

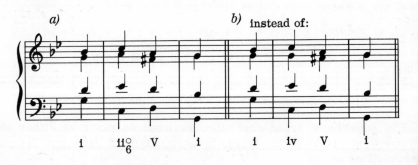

d) To prevent poor harmonic rhythm.

Fig. 15.17.

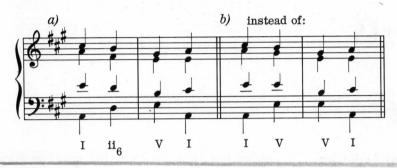

| I | ii$_6$ | V | I | | I | V | | V | I |

Chord Progression Review.

I: I–V, I–IV, I–vii^{o}, I–ii

V–I, IV–I, vii^{o}–I, ii$_6$–I$_6^4$

ii: ii–vii^{o}, ii–V, ii$_6$–I$_6^4$

I–ii

IV: IV–V, IV–I, IV–vii^{o}

I–IV

V: V–I

ii–V, IV–V, I–V

vii^{o}: vii^{o}–I

I–vii^{o}, ii–vii^{o}, IV–vii^{o}

Assignment 76. Harmonize melodies using the supertonic triad. Review pages 156-159 for writing a bass line using inversions. Keep in mind especially

a) the alternate doublings of the ii triad in a major key,

b) the fact that ii^{o} in a minor key can be used only in first inversion (ii$_6^{o}$).

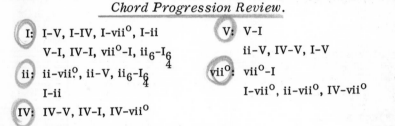

(1)

(2)

(3)

(4)

Assignment 77. Write original exercises including examples of the supertonic triad. Follow directions in Assignment 70.

EAR TRAINING AND MUSIC READING

Exercise 90. Singing the supertonic triad.

a) In a major key: Sing the tonic triad of the given key; sing the supertonic note and sing the ii triad with letter names.

b) In a minor key: Sing the tonic triad of the given key; sing the supertonic note and the ii° triad with letter names.

c) Same as b) but sing the ii triad.

Exercise 91. Sing with letter names each of the following chord progressions in the given key.

<blockquote>
Major key: I ii V I; I ii vii^o I

Minor key: i ii° V i; i ii vii^o I
</blockquote>

Example: i ii° V i in F minor

Fig. 15.18.

F A♭ C A♭ F   G B♭ D♭ B♭ G   C E G E C   F A♭ C A♭ F

Exercise 92. Harmonic dictation exercises will now include the supertonic triads studied in this chapter.

Caution should be taken not to confuse the first inversion of the supertonic triad with the subdominant triad, root in bass. Both triads have the *same bass tone* and both normally progress to V. Correct identification of the type of triad (minor or diminished) will aid in naming the triad correctly.

Fig. 15.19.

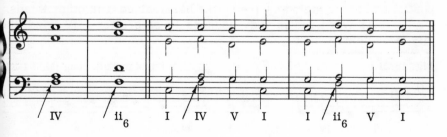

IV   ii₆   I IV V I   I ii₆ V I

Self-Help in Harmonic Dictation

The following excerpts from hymns contain only triads studied thus far.

Italian Hymn	1- 3	M- 2	Louvan	13-16	M-307
Tappan	8-10	M-61	Pleyel's Hymn	1- 8	M-326
Creation	1- 4	M-66, E-309	Pleyel's Hymn	1- 2	E-578
Tallis' Canon	5- 6	M-74, E-165	St. Agnes	1- 4	M-341, E- 24
Yorkshire	21-24	M-93, E- 16	Bristol	1- 2	E- 7
Uxbridge	1- 3, 10-12,	M-186	Spanish Chant	13-16	E-332
Gethsemane	9-12	M-207			

KEYBOARD HARMONY

Exercise 93. a) Play the progression I ii$_6$ V I in all major keys.
   b) Play the progression i ii$^\circ_6$ V i in all minor keys.
   c) Play the progression I ii$_6$ I$_6$ in all major keys and i ii$^\circ_6$ i$^6_4$
V i in all minor keys.

Fig. 15.20.

$$\text{I} \quad \text{ii}_6 \quad \text{V} \quad \text{I} \qquad \text{i} \quad \text{ii}^\circ_6 \quad \text{V} \quad \text{i} \qquad \text{i} \quad \text{ii}^\circ_6 \quad \text{i}^6_4 \quad \text{V} \quad \text{i}$$

Harmonizing a melody at the keyboard. The vii° triad and the ii or ii° triad can be found useful in harmonizing a melody at the keyboard in two different ways.

   a) Although most melodies can be harmonized with I, IV and V, portions of some melodies are better harmonized with other triads.
   (1) When the melody ascends by step after a IV triad, the vii$^\circ_6$ is ordinarily used.

Fig. 15.21.   Russian Folk Song (MSS I-37)

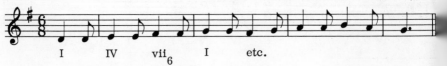

$$\text{I} \qquad \text{IV} \qquad \text{vii}_6 \qquad \text{I} \qquad \text{etc.}$$

(2) When the melody outlines a supertonic triad, the same triad is ordinarily found in the harmonization.

Fig. 15.22.   Haydn, Symphony in G Major, No. 100 (MSS I-179)

In the above example, the melody at "ii" outlines a ii triad and therefore cannot be harmonized by I, IV or V.

(b) The vii° and ii (or ii°) triads can often be used to give variety to a harmonization, instead of using only I, IV and V.

Fig. 15.23.   German Folk Song (MSS I-72)

Harmonizations can also be made more interesting through use of inversions—the first inversion during the course of the phrase and the I_6^4 at the cadence.

Exercise 94. Harmonize at the keyboard the following melodies, occasionally using vii°, ii or ii° in place of one of the three principal triads.

Music for Sight Singing, Part I - 37*, 45, 50*, 78*, 109, 178, 179;

Part II - 5*, 10, 23, 42, 55*, 62, 75, 81.

Exercise 95. Play examples from Assignments 73 and 75 at the keyboard.

---

*Particularly for the use of vii°.

16

The Melodic Line (II)

THEORY AND ANALYSIS

More advanced study of the melodic line will include expansion o
the materials of form already studied, more freedom in the use o
intervals, and consideration of the harmonic and non-harmonic val
ues of each melody note.

Form. A phrase of music may be lengthened by extension
thereby avoiding the monotony of a constant succession of regular
phrase lengths. Several ways of accomplishing this are illustrated
below.

a) Repeating a part of a phrase

Fig. 16.1.   French Folk Song (MSS I-99

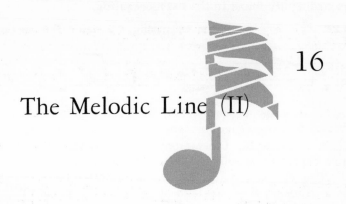

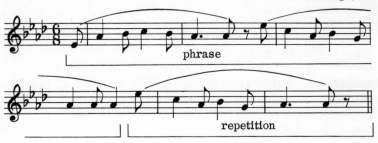

Exact repetition of an entire phrase is not extension. Since a phrase
and its repetition are considered a single phrase, they cannot b
considered as a period.

b) Evading the cadence at the end of the phrase, allowing th
melody to continue further to the ultimate cadence

Fig. 16.2.   French Folk Song (MSS I-47)

cadence evaded   extension

Without the evasion and extension, the phrase might have appeared
as a normal four-measure phrase.

Fig. 16.3.

(c) Using a sequential pattern during the course of the phrase

Fig. 16.4.   English Folk Song (MSS II-40)

Contrasting period:

phrase, 4 measures

extensions

by sequence

phrase, 6 measures

Without the two measures of sequence, the consequent phrase would
be a normal four-measure phrase.

Fig. 16.5.

    d) Lengthening a motive

Fig. 16.6.   German Folk Song (MSS I-36

                    one measure extra length

    e) Adding an additional motive to the phrase

Fig. 16.7.   German Folk Song (MSS I-57

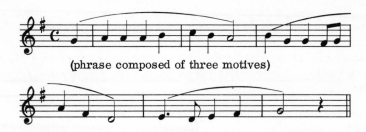

        (phrase composed of three motives)

    f) Occasionally phrases may be more or less than four meas-
ures in length. The following is a six-measure phrase, made up o
two three-measure motives.

Fig. 16.8.   Russian Folk Song (MSS I-78

All of the above illustrations are parts of complete periods. The
student should study the whole melody in each instance, and note
particularly that the other phrase of the period is often normal.

The two following forms are larger than the period.

    a) The *phrase group* consists of three or more phrases (very
often three) each of which differs melodically from the others. Usually, each of the first two phrases ends with a half cadence or an
imperfect cadence and the last phrase ends with a perfect cadence.

Fig. 16.9.   Mendelssohn, *Das Schifflein* (MSS I-181

                  phrase 1

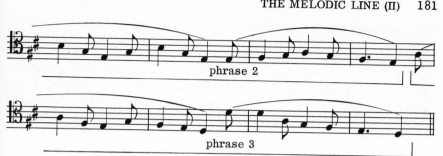

Any or all phrases of a phrase group may be lengthened by extension.

b) The *double period* consists of four phrases. Each of the
first three phrases ends with a semi-cadence, the last with a perfect cadence. Phrases one and three are usually similar to each
other and very often identical, or nearly so, as in Figure 16.10. A
form consisting of four different phrases (quite common in folk music) may be considered either as a double period or as a phrase
group.

Fig. 16.10.   Mendelssohn, *Venetianisches Gondellied,*
                           Op. 57, No. 5

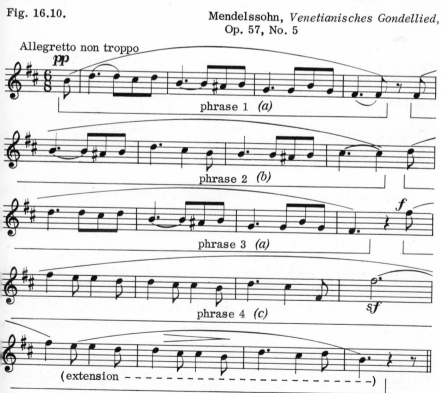

This example can be analyzed conveniently by assigning alphabet letters to each of the four phrases, the same letter for identical or nearly identical phrases and different letters for differing phrases. Thus the melody can be analyzed as *a b a c* since the first and third phrases are identical, and the second and fourth phrases differ from *a* and from each other. In cases where phrases are nearly alike, the prime symbol (´) is used with the repeated letter. For example, see *Music for Sight Singing,* Part I, Number 61, which is a double period *a b a b'*; the first and third phrases are identical while the second and fourth phrases are nearly identical.

No two successive phrases are identical in the double period, since simple phrase repetition would result. A melody analyzed as *a a b c* would be a phrase group, as *a* is simply a repeated phrase and not a period. (See *Music for Sight Singing,* Part II, No. 74.)

Any or all phrases of the double period may be found with extensions or in irregular lengths, as described previously.

Intervals. Intervals of a third or larger have been studied as specific leaps in the tonic, dominant and subdominant triads. Such intervals may be used in melodic writing in at least four additional ways.

a) The interval or intervals outline a chord other than I, IV or V.

Fig. 16.11.   Haydn, Symphony in G Major, No. 100
                                                    (MSS I-179)

b) Each note of the interval represents a different chord (a chord change occurs as the interval is sounded).

Fig. 16.12.   Mexican Folk Song (MSS II-65)

Two such leaps in the same direction are ordinarily not written (but see melody Number 61 in Part II of *Music for Sight Singing*).

c) The interval is a leap from a chord tone to a non-harmonic tone (or, less often, in the case of an escaped tone, a leap from a non-harmonic tone to a chord tone).

'ig. 16.13.   English Folk Song (MSS II-78)

d) The interval is found in a melodic sequence.

'ig. 16.14.   Brahms, *Vergebliches Ständchen* (MSS I-202)

See also melodies I - 180, 182; II - 67, 81)

Harmonic and Non-harmonic Values of Melodic Tones.   It should
)e possible to analyze each note of a melody in light of the following
:onsiderations and as shown in Figures 16.13 and 16.14.

a) Each note of the melody must be either part of a specific
riad or a non-harmonic tone to a triad.

b) The harmony implied by the melody must consist of a chord
;uccession based upon principles of chord succession and harmonic
·hythm already studied.

Assignment 78. Copy out melodies from *Music for Sight Singing*
.nd analyze the form of each.   Indicate the following, using Figure
.6.4 as a guide.

a) The beginning and ending of each phrase

b) The form of the entire melody (contrasting period, phrase,
;roup, and so on)

c) The location of any extensions and a description of each

d) The location of any phrases other than of four-measure
ength

Also analyze the harmonic background and identify non-harmonic
ones as in Figures 16.13-16.14.

Melodies: Part I - 35, 50, 74, 82, 87, 103, 108, 140, 146, 191.

Part II - 57, 90, 91, 93, 99.

APPLICATION

VRITTEN MATERIALS

Assignment 79.   Write original melodies in various forms as as-
;igned. Use extensions as studied in this chapter.   Make a *complete*

analysis of each melody you write. This will include *a*) an analysis
of form as in Figure 16.4 and *b*) a harmonic analysis as in Figures
16.13-16.14.

EAR TRAINING AND MUSIC READING

Sight singing and melodic dictation materials presented up to this
point have included only those intervals found in the three principal
triads. These intervals are the ones most often used in melodic
writing, but often found in contexts other than the three principal
triads.

Chapters 8a and 13a in *Music for Sight Singing* present examples
of such melodic writing. Study the prefatory material to Chapter 8.

The following exercises will aid in singing these intervals in
their new contexts.

Exercise 96. Singing individual scale tones. No note of the scale
is more than a whole step away from one of the notes of the tonic
triad (Figure 16.15 *a*). Choose a note of the scale, play the tonic
note of the key, sing the tonic triad and finally sing the chosen note.
Example (Figure 16.15 *b*): Sing A in the key of C.

Fig. 16.15.

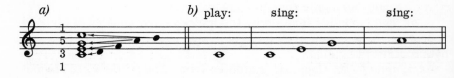

Exercise 97. Singing intervals. Figure 16.16 lists all the possible diatonic intervals (thirds through sevenths) in the key of C.
Select the interval to be sung. Play the tonic note of the key, find
the first note of the interval as in exercise 96 and sing the interval.

For adequate practice, Figure 16.16 should be copied in several
other keys. In minor keys, use the lowered sixth and raised seventh
scale steps.

Fig. 16.16.

Major and minor thirds

Exercise 98. Melodic dictation. After having practiced sight singing as outlined above, take comparable melodies from dictation, paying particular attention to those intervals not found in the three principal triads.

17

The Submediant
and Mediant Triads

THEORY AND ANALYSIS

The two remaining secondary triads are built on the submediant and mediant tones of the scale; both are minor triads (vi and iii) when found in a major key (Figure 17.1 *a*) and both are major triads (VI and III) when found in a minor key (Figure 17.1 *b*). Because of the altered sixth and seventh degrees in the minor scale, two additional triads are possible in a minor key. These are the vi° and the III+, diminished and augmented triads (Figure 17.1 *c*). Because of the infrequent use of the two latter triads, they will not be considered in this chapter.

Fig. 17.1.

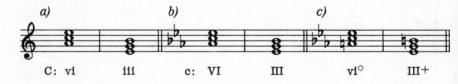

C: vi   iii   c: VI   III   vi°   III+

Assignment 80. Spelling the submediant and mediant triads.
  a) Spell the submediant triad in each major and minor key.
  b) Spell the mediant triad in each major and minor key.

The Submediant Triad

The submediant triad is commonly found in these progressions.

Major Key		Minor Key	
I - vi	vi - IV	i - VI	VI - iv
V - vi	vi - ii	V - VI	VI - ii$^{o}_{6}$
	vi - V		VI - V

When the progression V - vi or V - VI occurs at a cadence point, it is known as a *deceptive cadence*. The reason for the name becomes obvious from study of Figure 17.2. In each cadence, the V triad seems to demand resolution to the tonic triad, but instead the submediant triad is found as the resolution. (Note carefully that the first phrase of Figure 17.2 is in the key of F, while the second phrase is in the key of C.)

Fig. 17.2.[1] V - vi   Bach, *Heilig, heilig* (#235)

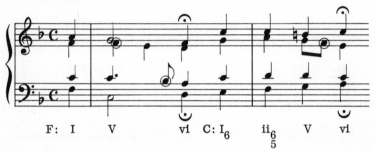

F: I   V   vi C: I$_6$ ii$_6$$_5$ V   vi

Other typical examples showing uses of the submediant triad are

Fig. 17.3. i - VI - iv   C. H. Graun (1701-1759) *Der Tod Jesu*

i   VI   iv

See also "America," measure 3.

---

[1] ii$_6$$_5$ = ii^7 in first inversion. See Chapter 20.

Fig. 17.4. vi - ii₆   Schubert, *Die Winterreise* "Frühlingstraum"

The Mediant Triad

The mediant triad is commonly found in these progressions.

Major Key		*Minor Key*	
I - iii	iii - IV	i - III	III - iv
	iii - vi		
vi - iii (in the progression		VI - III (in the progression	
vi - iii - IV)		VI - III - iv)	

Fig. 17.5. i - III - iv₆   Bach, *Jesu, meine Freude* (#138)

The progression iii - IV or III - iv is particularly useful in harmonizing the descending scale (major or minor). The mediant triad
may be used to harmonize the descending leading tone. Figure 17.6 *a*
shows the complete E♭ major scale harmonized using the iii - IV
progression. This scale could have begun with a tonic triad, as
shown in Figure 17.6 *b*.

Fig. 17.6. Mendelssohn, *Christus*

The progression iii - vi (Figure 17.7) is not as commonly used as the previous progressions. In a minor key, the progression III - VI is only rarely used.

Fig. 17.7. iii - vi Wagner, *Lohengrin* (Act III)

A rather frequent cadence device is a vertical sonority which can be spelled as a mediant triad and occurs immediately preceding the tonic triad of the cadence. In reality, it is a dominant triad with a non-harmonic tone in the soprano voice (or, more rarely, in an inner voice).

Fig. 17.8. Hymn: Hamburg

At the * the triad can be spelled A C E, which would be iii in F major. But because of the cadence, it is more logical to consider the A to be an upper neighbor to the V triad. The aural effect, at this point, is certainly that of an authentic cadence.

In a similar situation in a minor key (Figure 17.9), the sonority at the * is spelled A♭ C E, an augmented triad, III+ in the key of F minor. Again the aural effect of the authentic cadence indicates that the A♭ in the soprano is a non-harmonic tone, this time an appoggiatura.

Fig. 17.9.   Melchior Vulpius (1560-1616) *Der Tag bricht an*

The figured bass 6 5 is used to indicate this cadence.

Fig. 17.10.

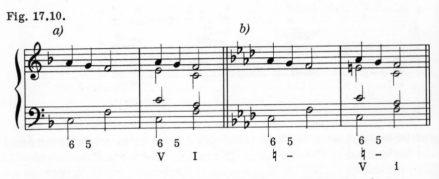

This progression (V₆ ₅ - I) can also be found within the phrase.

The submediant and mediant triads are less commonly used in inversion, for example, in a series of first inversions.

Fig. 17.11.   Bach, *Jesu Leiden, Pein und Tod* (#106)

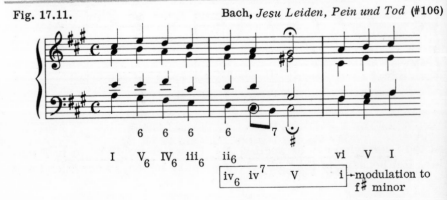

Special Use of the Tonic Triad in a Chord Progression

The tonic triad is often found between the two triads of a commonly used progression. In Figure 17.12, placing the tonic triad between vi and IV only temporarily interrupts a normal chord progression. Such placement of a tonic chord can be made between the two triads of any progression studied thus far, for example, ii - I - V, iii - I - IV, and so on.

Fig. 17.12.   Bach, *Wie schön leuchtet der Morgenstern* (#323)

vi   I₆   IV

Assignment 81.   Analyze the harmony and non-harmonic tones of the following excerpts.

Mozart, Sonatas for Piano
    C Major, K. 545, second movement, measures 12-16,
                        third movement, measures 1-8
    B♭ Major, K. 333, third movement, measures 13-16
    D Major, K. 284, third movement, variation 11, measures 1-3
    D Major, K. 311, second movement, last 8 measures
Schumann, *Album for the Young,* Op. 68
    No. 9, measures 1-4; No. 37, measures 9-16
Mendelssohn, *Songs Without Words,* No. 7 (Op. 30, No. 1), measures 1-6
Murphy and Melcher, *Music for Study,* Chapters 11, 12, 14.

APPLICATION

WRITTEN MATERIALS

The Submediant Triad

Part-writing procedures previously presented can be used in these progressions.

Rule 2A or 2B: vi - ii. See Figures 17.13 *a, b* and 17.14.

Rule 3: V - vi. See Figures 17.13 *c* and 17.2.
    vi - V. See Figure 17.13 *d.*

Rule 5: V - vi. See Figures 17.13 *e* and 17.2.
    V - VI. See Figures 17.15 and 17.16.

Rule 6A: Any progression in which one triad is in inversion.
    See Figure 17.4.

Fig. 17.13.

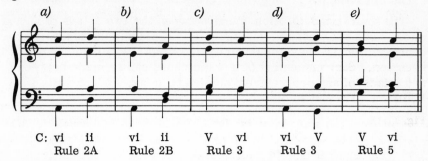

Fig. 17.14. vi - ii   Johann Schein (1586-1630), *Ach lob den Herrn*

In a minor key, Rule 5 is used in the progression V - VI. Other-wise, in using Rule 3, the leading tone in the V triad will skip the interval of an augmented second to the root of the VI triad.

Fig. 17.15.

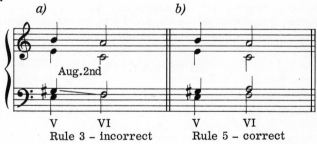

Fig. 17.16.   Bach, *Wer weiss, wie nahe mir* (#204)

The following progressions require new procedures.

a) vi - V (soprano descending); VI - V. In a major key (vi-V), Rule 3 will be used when the soprano moves opposite to the bass. A notable exception occurs in other situations. When the soprano moves in similar motion with the bass in either major or minor, Rule 5 is not effective, since either a doubled leading tone, an augmented second, or both, will result. (See Figure 17.17 *a*). In addition, in the progression VI - V (in minor), no matter what motion between soprano and bass is used, parallel fifths, octaves, augmented seconds and/or doubled leading tone will result (see Figure 17.17 *b, c*) whether Rule 3 or 5 is used.

Fig. 17.17.

To avoid these difficulties, the third of the submediant triad is doubled (see Figure 17.18). Each of the two triads involved (dominant and submediant) shows the same doubling whether the progression is V - VI or VI - V, so no new rule is presented.

Fig. 17.18.   Bach, *Herzliebster Jesu, was hast du* (#78)

b) I - vi (in major); i - VI (in minor); vi - IV (in major); VI - iv (in minor). In these progressions, the roots of the two triads in the bass are the interval of a third apart.

Part-Writing Rule 4A. When the bass notes of two successive triads are roots of the triads and these triad roots are a third apart, hold the two common tones and move the other voice stepwise.

Fig. 17.19.

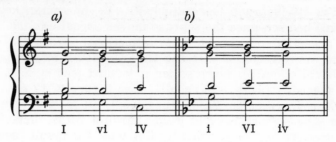

See also Figure 17.3. This rule is also used to write the progression IV - ii.

Part-Writing Rule 4B. When the bass notes of two successive
triads are roots of triads and these triad roots are a third apart
move the three upper voices contrary to the bass. See also Figure
15.2 (IV - ii).

Fig. 17.20.   Mendelssohn, *St. Paul*

Rule 5 is sometimes used in place of Rule 4B. In Figure 17.21
doubling the third in the vi triad (a minor triad, the third of which is
the tonic note) helps to keep the tenor voice in its normal range.

Fig. 17.21.   Mendelssohn, *Elijah*

c) vi - IV$_6$. The use of a passing tone with the vi triad to
create a IV$_6$ triad structure on the second half of the beat is shown

in Figure 17.22. The vi triad is found here with a doubled third, allowing the IV_6 triad to be found with normal doubling (soprano
doubled in first inversion).

Fig. 17.22.   Bach, *Alle Menschen müssen sterben* (#153)

I   vi(IV_6)I_6

Assignment 82. Write deceptive cadences by filling in the inner
voices (numbers 1-10) or supplying the three upper voices (numbers
11-15). Make a harmonic analysis of each exercise. In this assignment, the last triad of each example is the submediant triad.

Assignment 83. Write exercises showing uses of the submediant triad other than the deceptive cadence. Fill in inner voices and make a harmonic analysis of each example.

The Mediant Triad

No new procedures are needed to write progressions using the mediant triad.

Rules 2A, 2B and 2C: iii - vi. See Figure 17.7.

vi - iii, VI - III. See Figures 17.6 and 17.9.

Rule 3:   iii - IV, III - iv. See Figure 17.6.

Rule 4A or 4B: I - iii, i - III. See Figure 17.5.

Rule 6A: Any progression in which one triad is in inversion. See Figure 17.5. This includes the mediant triad at the cadence. See Figures 17.8-17.9.

Assignment 84. Write exercises showing uses of the mediant triad. Fill in inner voices and make a harmonic analysis of each example.

(12)

6   6   6 5   ♮   –

Assignment 85. Write extended exercises, making use of both the submediant and mediant triads. Fill in inner voices and make a harmonic analysis of each example.

Assignment 86. Harmonize the following melodies from hymn, chorale and folk sources, using the submediant and mediant triads. Make harmonic analysis. Indicate tempo and dynamics.

Assignment 87. Write original exercises for voices or instruments in forms assigned by instructor. Make harmonic analysis. Indicate tempo and dynamic markings.

Chord Progression Review

 I: I may progress to any triad

     Any triad may progress to I (review page 191)

ii: ii-vii^{o}, ii-V, ii$_6$-I$_4$

     I-ii, vi-ii, IV-ii

iii: iii-vi, iii-IV

      I-iii, vi-iii (in vi-iii-IV)

IV: IV-I, IV-ii, IV-V, IV-vii^{o}

     I-IV, vi-IV, iii-IV

 V: V-I , V-vi

     I-V, ii-V, IV-V, vi-V

vi: vi-ii, vi-IV, vi-V, vi-iii (in vi-iii-IV)

     I-vi, iii-vi, V-vi

vii^{o}: vii^{o}-I

       I-vii^{o}, ii-vii^{o}, IV-vii^{o}

EAR TRAINING AND MUSIC READING

Exercise 99. Singing the submediant triad.   Sing with letter names the tonic triad of the given key.   Find the submediant note by singing a minor third below the tonic in a major key, or by singing a major third below the tonic in a minor key.   Sing the submediant triad with letter names.   (See Figure 17.23 *a, b.*)

Exercise 100. Singing the mediant triad. Follow directions given in Exercise 99, but find the mediant note by singing a major third above the tonic in a major key, or a minor third above the tonic in a minor key.   (See Figure 17.23 *c, d.*)

Fig. 17.23.

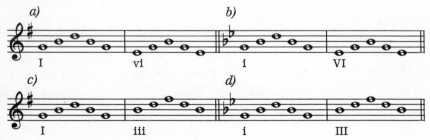

Exercise 101. Sing with letter names each of the following chord progressions in keys given by instructor.

Major key: I vi ii. V I   I iii IV V I

             I vi V I

             I vi IV V I

             I V vi

Minor key: i VI iv V i   i III iv V i

             i VI ii° V i

             i VI V i

             i V VI

Follow example as given in Figure 15.18.

Exercise 102. Harmonic dictation. Harmonic dictation will now include the submediant and mediant triads. The most common uses of these triads, and therefore the ones to be found most often in the dictation exercises, will be those in the progressions in Exercise 101. Other uses of these triads may be added as the progressions are studied in part-writing.

Self-Help in Harmonic Dictation

The Submediant Triad

Hail, Thou Star	1–8	G–73	Varina	1–4	M–523
Irish	1–7	M–14	Weimar	1–4	E–37
		E–444	Jervaulx Abbey	1–3	E–128
Ratisbon	1–4	M–32	All Saints	1–2	E–130
		E–153	Riley	1–4	E–292
Joanna	5–6	M–64	St. Denio	1–4	E–301
Dundee (French)	1–4	M–68	Deus Tuorum Militum	1–4	E–344
St. Cross	1–2	M–134			
Hanover	1–4	M–169			
		E–288			
Orientis Partibus	1–4	M–437			

The Mediant Triad

St. Magnus	5–8	M–163	Knickerbocker	1–3	E–207
		E–106	Riley	13–16	E–292
Lenox	11–15	M–189			

KEYBOARD HARMONY

Exercise 103. *a)* Play the deceptive cadence in each major and minor key. In major, when the melody line between V and vi descends, use part-writing Rule 3; when melody line ascends; use Rule 5. In minor, always use Rule 5.

Fig. 17.24.

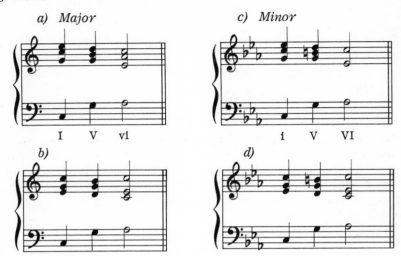

b) Practice at the keyboard the part-writing exercises in Assignments 82-83.

Exercise 104. Play chord progressions using the submediant and mediant triads. As with previous keyboard exercises, all the following progressions can be played in close position, using three notes in the right hand and one in the left, and following correct part-writing procedure from triad to triad. Although illustration of all possible progressions would consume too much space, two typical examples follow.

Fig. 17.25.

a) Play the following progressions in any or all keys, as assigned.

not C

Major keys ·

I vi ii V I	I iii IV V (or vii$^{O}_{6}$) I
✓ I vi IV V (or vii$^{O}_{6}$) I	I iii vi ii V I
I vi V I	I iii vi IV V (or vii$^{O}_{6}$) I
I vi ii$_{6}$ V I	I V vi iii IV V (or vii$^{O}_{6}$) I
I IV V vi	(opening tonic chord with
I ii$_{6}$ V vi	third in soprano)

B♭

not a

Minor keys,

i VI iv V i	i III iv V i
i VI ii$^{O}_{6}$ V i	i III VI iv V i
✓ i VI V i	i III VI ii$^{O}_{6}$ V i
i iv V VI	i V VI III iv V i
i ii$^{O}_{6}$ V VI	(opening tonic chord with
	third in soprano)

b) Play part-writing exercises in Assignments 84-85.

Harmonizing the Scale at the Keyboard. Enough harmonic vocabulary has now been acquired to harmonize major and minor scales, both ascending and descending. More than one harmonization is possible in each case. Examples of major and minor scales, using triads with roots in the bass, are written out. Other harmonizations are suggested by chord numbers.

Fig. 17.26. Major

I   V   I   IV   I   IV   vii$^{O}_{6}$ I   I   iii   IV   I   IV   I   V   I

3 keys
not C & G

* inversion necessary here

B♭, F, D

Fig. 17.27. Minor

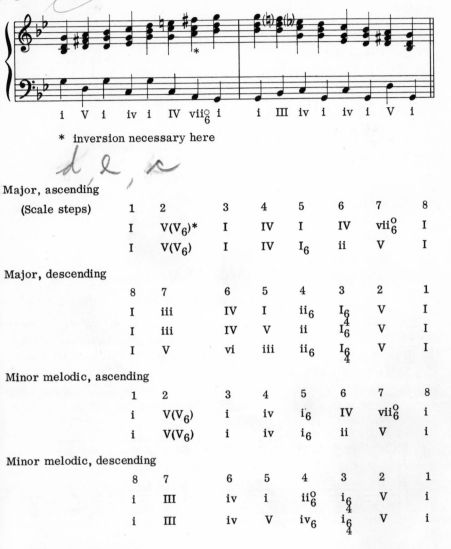

| | i | V | i | iv | i | IV | vii$^o_6$ | i | | i | III | iv | i | iv | i | V | i |

* inversion necessary here

Major, ascending

(Scale steps)	1	2	3	4	5	6	7	8
	I	V(V$_6$)*	I	IV	I	IV	vii$^o_6$	I
	I	V(V$_6$)	I	IV	I$_6$	ii	V	I

Major, descending

	8	7	6	5	4	3	2	1
	I	iii	IV	I	ii$_6$	I$_6$	V	I
	I	iii	IV	V	ii	I$^4_6$	V	I
	I	V	vi	iii	ii$_6$	I$_{6\ 4}$	V	I

Minor melodic, ascending

	1	2	3	4	5	6	7	8
	i	V(V$_6$)	i	iv	i$_6$	IV	vii$^o_6$	i
	i	V(V$_6$)	i	iv	i$_6$	ii	V	i

Minor melodic, descending

	8	7	6	5	4	3	2	1
	i	III	iv	i	ii$^o_6$	i$^4_6$	V	i
	i	III	iv	V	iv$_6$	i$_{6\ 4}$	V	i

Exercise 105. Play harmonized major and minor scales, ascending and descending, and with various triad progressions, as assigned.

---

*Triads in parenthesis are alternate harmonizations.

18

Miscellaneous Triad Usages

THEORY AND ANALYSIS

The v Triad in a Minor Key

The v (minor) triad is used instead of the V (major) triad when one of the melodic lines descends through the seventh scale step at the time a dominant triad is used. Observe the alto line in Figure 18.1 and the bass line in Figure 18.2.

Fig. 18.1.   Brahms, *Schnitter Tod*

Fig. 18.2.   Bach, *Jesu, meine Freude* (#263)

Assignment 88. Spell the minor dominant triad in each minor key.

Half Cadences

The V triad of the authentic half cadence may be preceded by triads other than I. These half cadences are commonly used.

Major key	ii–V	*Minor key*	ii$^o_6$–V
	IV–V		iv–V
	vi–V		

The half cadence iv–V in a minor key is often known as a *Phrygian cadence*. It is so named because in the progression iv$_6$ – V the bass descends one half step while an upper voice ascends one whole step (Figures 18.3 *a*, 18.4). This is characteristic of the Phrygian mode,[1] a medieval scale in which 1-2 is a half step and 7-8 is a whole step (Figure 18.3 *c*). In the cadence iv–V (Figure 18.3 *b*), the characteristic half step and whole step relationship is reversed.

Fig. 18.3.

Fig. 18.4.   Brahms, *Sankt Raphael*

---

[1]Mode is a term applied to various orderly arrangements of the diatonic scale (c d e f g a b c), particularly to scales of the medieval European era (see *Music for Sight Singing,* page 185). Major and minor scales are sometimes known as major and minor modes.

The Six-Four Chords (Triads in Second Inversion)

The *cadential six-four* chord has already been studied (review pages 107-108). It is by far the most frequently used of all the six-four chords. Thus far in our studies of it, the moving voices above the bass have proceeded downward. But occasionally the upper voices ascend after the tonic six-four.

Fig. 18.5.   Hymn: Mendelssohn

a) The Passing Six-Four. This six-four chord can be easily identified by the melodic pattern in the bass voice and one upper voice. As the bass ascends three scale steps, the other voice descends the same three scale steps (or the bass descends and the other voice ascends). The passing six-four chord will appear on the second of the three bass notes, passing between the two other chords.

Most common of the passing six-four chords is the passing V_4^6 found between two positions of the tonic triad.

Fig. 18.6.
    a)   b)

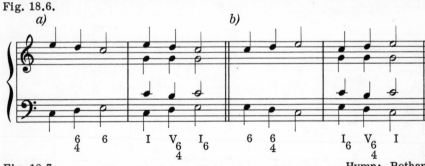

Fig. 18.7.   Hymn: Bethany

Passing six-four chords other than the V_6^4 and I_6^4 are uncommon,[2] though theoretically any triad can be found in second inversion as a passing chord. The following example shows the use of vi_6^4 between V and vii°.

Fig. 18.8.

Bach: *Herzlich tut mich verlangen* (#21)

vi   V V_4^2 vi_6^4 vii°$_6$ I_6 IV   I

b) The Pedal Six-Four.[3] Here the chord preceding the six-four has the same bass note as the six-four; the six-four usually resolves to the same triad which preceded it. The name derives from the pedal point effect in the bass. The pedal $_4^6$ is most commonly found in the pattern I - IV_6^4 - I.

Fig. 18.9.

Wagner, *Lohengrin* (Act 3)

Massig bewegt

p

I   I IV_6^4 -   I

c) The Arpeggiated Six-Four. Preceding this six-four chord is the same chord with root or third in the bass. The bass line shows an arpeggio effect.

---

[2]The passing I_6^4 is commonly used in the progression IV_6 - I_6^4 - ii_5^6 and will be considered in the study of seventh chords.
[3]Also known as an auxiliary six-four or an embellishing six-four.

Fig. 18.10.   Hymn: Beatitudo

APPLICATION

WRITTEN MATERIALS

No new procedures are necessary in writing the v triad.

In the Phrygian cadence the iv₆ is found with various doublings.

Fig. 18.11.

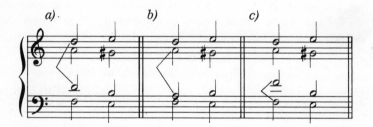

Examples of cadences in Figure 18.11 may be found as follows:

    a) Figure 18.4

    b) Bach chorale #292, second phrase

    c) Figure 19.13.

Assignment 89-90. Write examples of the v triad and of the Phrygian cadence. Fill in inner voices. Make harmonic analysis.

Assignment 89.

Assignment 90.

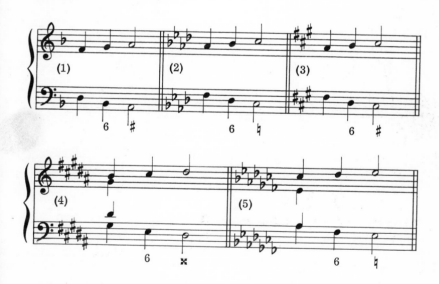

In writing any of the six-four chords, these two part-writing procedures usually apply.

a) Approach and Departure. The bass note of the six-four is preceded and followed only by

    (1) the same bass note

    (2) a note a step above or below

    (3) a skip in the *same* chord

(4) less commonly, a skip from the supertonic note, progression ii(ii^7)—I$_6$ (See Figure 20.16).
$\quad\quad\quad\quad\quad\quad\quad\quad\quad\quad\quad$ 4

b) Doubling. The bass note (fifth of the triad) is doubled.

Assignment 91. Write examples of the various uses of the six-four chord. Fill in inner voices and make harmonic analysis. In addition, identify the type of each six-four as cadential, passing, pedal or arpeggiated.

Assignment 92. Part-writing review. These exercises will contain examples of most part-writing procedures studied to date, including the six-four chords. Fill in inner voices and make harmonic analysis.

Assignment 93. Part-writing review. Bass voice only given.
Supply soprano voice, add inner parts and make harmonic analysis.

Assignment 94. Part-writing an unfigured bass. In this type of
problem, the bass line only is given, and without figuration. It must
be determined which triads are in inversion and which have the root

in the bass. Many solutions are possible for each exercise, so try
several and compare them with each other, finally selecting the
most musical. Below are three of the possible figurations for the
first two measures of the first exercise.

Fig. 18.12.

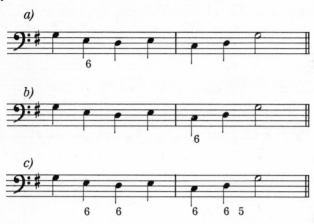

Assignment 94.

EAR TRAINING AND MUSIC READING

Exercise 106. Sing with letter names the progression i - v - i in each minor key.

Exercise 107. Harmonic dictation exercises will now include the chords and progressions studied in this chapter.

Self-Help in Harmonic Dictation

Phrygian Cadence			*v Triad*		
Leoni	1-2	M-5, E-285	Old Hundred Twelfth	1-6	E-225
Heinlein	1-2	E-55			
Babylon's Streams	1-2	E-60			

KEYBOARD HARMONY

Exercise 108. Play at the keyboard the progressions in Assignments 89-91.

Exercise 109. Play the descending minor scale as follows:

8	7	6	5	4	3	2	1
i	v	VI	III	iv(ii$_6^0$)	i$_6^4$	V	i

Melody Harmonization at the Keyboard. Using keyboard procedures previously learned, melodies may be harmonized using the harmonic materials learned in Chapters 17 and 18. The following example shows a keyboard harmonization using vi and at the cadence the V triad with the 6 5 melody line.

Fig. 18.13.   French Folk Song (MSS I-44)

Exercise 110. Harmonize melodies at the keyboard from the list below, as assigned. In the following melodies from *Music for Sight Singing,* it is possible to use the triads or progressions as indicated.

a) (1) The vi triad (major keys). Part I - 11, 22, 31, 33, 35, 37, 38, 40, 44, 68, 72, 80, 88, 105, 111, 123, 127, 129, 131, 143, 150, 167, 172, 178, 194; Part II - 1, 9, 15, 22, 23, 28, 40, 43, 56.

(2) The VI triad (minor keys). Part I - 41, 59, 115; Part II - 11, 47, 55.

b) The iii triad (major keys). Part I - 11, 40, 57, 105, 106, 113, 132, 135; Part II - 5, 12, 21, 24, 40, 74.

c) (1) The deceptive cadence - major keys. Part I - 13, 39, 102, 140; Part II - 18.

(2) The deceptive cadence - minor keys. Part I - 41, 104.

d) (1) The V with 6 5 soprano, major keys. Part I - 15, 16, 32, 37, 44, 47, 106, 129, 141; Part II - 7.

(2) The V with 6 5 soprano, minor keys. Part I - 53, 86, 107; Part II - 42.

e) The v triad in minor. Part I - 121; Part II - 11.

f) The Phrygian cadence. Part I - 21, 41, 59; Part II - 31, 47.

19

Non-Harmonic Tones (II)

THEORY AND ANALYSIS

Figured Bass Symbols for Non-Harmonic Tones

There are no standard figured bass symbols for non-harmonic tones; symbols are used which will best express the particular musical situation at the time. Very often, two or more figures will be found under a single bass note. These will be read in the same manner as the figuration for second inversion, 6 5. Each horizontal
                                                4 3
line of figuration is read from left to right, indicating a melodic progression at the given interval above the bass. When the bass note changes, the number or numbers under the new bass note have no connection with the numbers under the previous bass note.

Fig. 19.1.

8 7 octave above bass (in tenor) moves to seventh above bass; at
6 5 the same time, sixth above bass (in soprano) moves to fifth
    above bass

5 6 7 - fifth above bass (in tenor) moves to sixth, then to seventh
3 - - 4 above bass; dash (-) indicates previous number to be held; at
  the same time, third above bass (in soprano) is held while
  tenor moves, after which soprano moves to fourth above
  bass

Basic Procedure for Use of Non-Harmonic Tones

Whether writing, analyzing, playing or listening to non-harmonic
tones, one basic concept should be kept in mind—*When a non-har-*
monic tone is used, it temporarily replaces a harmonic tone.

Fig. 19.2.

In Figure 19.2 *a*, the passing tone D in the bass temporarily replaces the note C, the root of the triad. In Figure 19.2 *b*, the suspension G in the alto temporarily replaces the note F♯, the third of
the triad. When the suspended G resolves, the triad is found with
normal doubling—two roots, one third and one fifth. Note that ordinarily an unaccented non-harmonic tone replaces the tone which
preceded it, as in the passing tone above; an accented non-harmonic
tone replaces the tone which follows it, as in the suspension above.

Single Non-Harmonic Tones

Single non-harmonic tones have been described in Chapter 13.
Further description is unnecessary except for suspensions. These
are of several varieties, each identified by the figured bass symbol
usually associated with it.

In any of the suspensions, the note of approach is usually at least
as long as the suspended note itself. The note of approach may be
twice as long as the suspended note, or the same length as the suspended note, but rarely (in four-part vocal style) shorter than the
suspended note.

a) The 4 3 suspension

Fig. 19.3.   Bach, *Ermuntre dich, mein schwacher Geist* (#102)

The suspended note G in the tenor temporarily replaces the following note F♯. At the resolution, the triad has normal doubling—two
roots, one third, one fifth.

b) The 7 6 suspension

Fig. 19.4.   Bach, *Auf meinen lieben Gott* (#304)

The suspended note is found in the viiₒ triad. With the fifth in the
soprano, the normal doubling is two fifths, one root and one third.
Here the suspended note temporarily replaces the root (F♯).
Normal doubling is found at the point of resolution.

c) The 9 8 suspension

Fig. 19.5.   Haydn, *Missa Sanctae Caecilae*

When this suspension is found in the tenor voice at an interval of
a second above the bass voice, it is known as a 2 1 suspension.

Fig. 19.6.   Bach, *Jesu, geh'voran*

(d) The 5 suspension (sometimes known as the 2 3 suspension)
      2

This suspension is always found in the bass voice, the necessary
figuration 5 giving its name.   Since the suspended note in the bass
             2

temporarily replaces the third of the triad, the upper voices show
normal doubling for first inversion.   The alternate name 2 3 derives
from the fact that the interval of a second at the point of suspension
resolves to the interval of a third.

Fig. 19.7.   Bach, *Liebster Jesu, wir sind hier* (#131)

(e) The 5 4 suspension.
This suspension occurs in a tonic six-four chord.

Fig. 19.8.   Bach, *Als der gütige Gott* (#159)

f) The 9, 7, and 4 suspensions

These suspensions are identical with the 9 8, 7 6 and 4 3 suspensions, except that at the moment of resolution of the suspended note, there is a change of structure in the harmony—either another inversion of the chord, or a different chord. The 9 suspension is the most common of the three.

Change of inversion

Fig. 19.9.   Bach, *Befiehl du deine Wege* (#367)

Change of harmony

Fig. 19.10.   Bach, *Meinen Jesum lass' ich nicht* (#152)

g) Suspensions with ornamental resolutions. These are of two varieties.

(1) The note of suspension skips down to another tone, usually either a third (non-harmonic) or a fourth (harmonic) before proceeding to its resolution.

Fig. 19.11.   Bach, *Liebster Jesu, wir sind hier* (#328)

(2) The note of resolution is followed by a lower neighboring tone.

Fig. 19.12.   Bach, *Heilig bist du Herr Gott Zebaoth*

The G in the tenor is merely decorative. The tenor C could have been held through three eighth notes.

(h) The chain suspension

A chain suspension occurs when two or more suspensions follow each other in succession and when the note of resolution of one suspension becomes the note of approach for the next suspension.

Fig. 19.13.   Bach, *Was betrübst du dich, mein Herze* (#237)

Two or three suspensions in a chain is the usual number. For a chain of five suspensions, see chorale number 168 *(Heut' ist, o Mensch)*.

Ambiguous Non-Harmonic Passages

In some passages involving non-harmonic tones, the location and description of the non-harmonic tone and the analysis of the surrounding harmony can be considered in more than one way.

Fig. 19.14.   Bach, *Herzliebster Jesu, was hast du* (#59)

etc.

At the mark (*), the sonority might be considered as
   a) ii^7 (A C E$\flat$ G) followed by iv$_6$ (C E$\flat$ G)
   b) ii^7 with G in tenor as lower neighboring tone
   c) iv with A in tenor as accented passing tone
   In situations such as this, it is not necessary to find the single correct analysis. The only objective of musical analysis is the description of the musical situation as it exists. When more than one possibility of analysis exists, this should be recognized. In subsequent chapters, other musical situations will be presented in which no single correct analysis will be possible.

Multiple Non-Harmonic Tones

   Very often two non-harmonic tones, either two of the same kind or one each of two different kinds, are used simultaneously. Three non-harmonic tones can also be used simultaneously, but this practice is less common.
   a) *Double or triple non-harmonic tones of the same kind.* These are usually found in thirds and sixths with each other. Double passing tones are quite common; all other double and triple non-harmonic tones are much less common.
   Double passing tones. The first full measure of Figure 19.15 shows, on beat 2, double passing tones in thirds; on beat 3, double passing tones in tenths (a third plus an octave); on beat 4, double passing tones in sixths.

Fig. 19.15.   Bach, *Was mein Gott will* (#41)

5	6		7	6	6
3	4		4	6	5
3	—		3	3	2

Double passing tones in contrary motion

Fig. 19.16.   Bach, *Nun freut euch, lieben Christen g'mein*
(#183)

Double neighboring tones

Fig. 19.17.   Bach, *Aus meines Herzens Grunde* (#1)

Double suspension

Fig. 19.18.   Bach, *Es stehn vor Gottes Throne* (#166)

Double appoggiatura

Fig. 19.19.   Bach, *Nun ruhen alle Wälder* (#63)

Double anticipation

Fig. 19.20.   Bach, *Werde munter, mein Gemüte* (#121)

Triple appoggiatura

Fig. 19.21.   Bach, *Dir, dir, Jehovah, will ich singen* (#209)

Triple passing tones

Fig. 19.22.   Bach, *Hinunter ist der Sonnenschein*

b) *Different non-harmonic tones used in conjunction with each other.* Different non-harmonic tones used simultaneously can be found in many combinations. The following examples illustrate four of these.

Fig. 19.23.   Bach, *Ich steh an Deiner Krippen hier*

In the last measure of Figure 19.23, the soprano moves to a lower neighboring tone (A to G) while the alto holds a suspension G. Both non-harmonic tones resolve simultaneously.

Fig. 19.24.   Bach, *Werde munter, mein Gemüte* (#121)

Figure 19.24 illustrates the simultaneous use of a lower neighbor (alto voice) and a passing tone (tenor voice). Note also the double accented passing tones on the fourth beat of the measure.

At the cadence an anticipation in the soprano occurs simultaneously with a passing tone in the tenor. The combination of the two non-harmonic tones here produces perfect parallel fifths. (See also chorale number 8, third phrase.)

Fig. 19.25.   Bach, *O Jesu Christ, du höchstes Gut* (#92)

At the cadence in Figure 19.25, the escaped tone C♯ sounds simultaneously with the lower neighbor E in the bass.

The following excerpt shows a pedal point above which is a series of first inversions with non-harmonic tones in the soprano line.

Fig. 19.26.   Brahms, *Gypsy Songs* (No. 9)

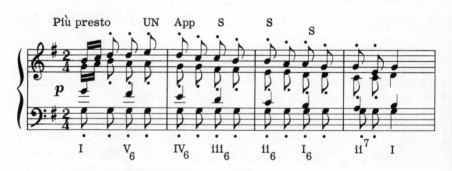

The *appoggiatura chord* is a name often given to a group of tones forming a chord but sounding over a bass note from a different chord. It is often found in keyboard music at a final cadence.

Fig. 19.27.   Beethoven, Sonata for Piano in A Major,
                                 Op. 2, No. 2, third movement

Chromatic Non-Harmonic Tones

Notes in music are often chromatically altered by placing an accidental before the note. This is done for one of five reasons.

a) To notate the various forms of the minor scale (raised
seventh degree in harmonic minor; raised sixth and seventh degrees
in melodic minor).

b) To alter a non-harmonic tone.

c) To alter a chord, for example, in F major, to alter the ii
triad (G B♭ D) to a II triad (G B D).

d) To indicate diatonic tones of the scale when the music is
written in a key other than that of the key signature.

e) To remind the performer of the proper accidental, even
when not actually necessary.

All the above uses are illustrated in the following excerpt.

Fig. 19.28.   Mozart, Sonata in F Major, K. 332

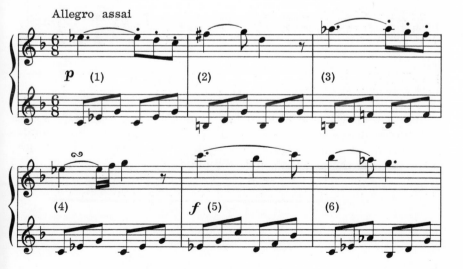

Measure 1. The key signature indicates F major, but the music is in the key of C minor. Therefore, E♭ and A♭ will need to be added. The E♭ appears in this measure.

Measure 2. The F♯ is an altered non-harmonic tone. It is an appoggiatura, altered from F to F♯. The B natural is raised from B♭ because of the use of the harmonic minor scale.

Measure 3. The natural sign before the F is not required, but is placed as a reminder to the performer because F♯ has been sounded in the previous measure.

Measure 7. The F♯ is part of an altered chord, D F♯ A♭ C (a French sixth, to be studied later).

Of these five uses of altered tones, the second will be the concern of the following material.

Fig. 19.29.   Verdi, *Aida,* Act II

At the sign (*), the altered upper neighboring tone, C♭, sounds simultaneously with the suspension E♭ in the alto. This complex combination of tones results in a vertical structure, F A♭, C♭ E♭, at the point of the altered non-harmonic tone.

Fig. 19.30.   Bach, *Verleih' uns Frieden gnädiglich* (#91)

At the sign (*) the A♯ in the tenor is an altered passing tone, sounding simultaneously with the passing tone E in the alto. In this example, no new chord structure is formed at the point of the altered non-harmonic tone, thus it is a truly dissonant altered non-harmonic tone.

Spelling the altered non-harmonic tone. Altered non-harmonic tones are usually spelled according to the direction in which the non-harmonic tone resolves. When the non-harmonic tone resolves *upwards* it takes the letter name *below* the harmonic tone to which it resolves. In the Bach example above, the altered passing tone progresses up to B, and is spelled A♯ rather than B♭. (See also Figure 19.28, measure 2.) When the non-harmonic tone resolves *down* it takes the letter name *above* the harmonic tone to which it progresses. In Figure 19.29, C♭ resolves down to B♭.

Composers often show a lack of consistency in spelling altered non-harmonic tones, as shown in the two excerpts following.

Fig. 19.31.   Chopin, *Waltz*, Op. 64, No. 2

Fig. 19.32.   Chopin, *Waltz*, Op. 69, No. 1

At the sign (*) in the *Waltz*, Op. 64, the descending altered passing tone takes the letter name *above* the tone to which it resolves (B$\flat\flat$ to A$\flat$). At the sign (*) in the *Waltz*, Op. 69, No. 1, the descending altered passing tone takes the *same* letter name as the tone to which it resolves (E natural to E$\flat$).

The student is urged to study the chorale harmonizations of Johann Sebastian Bach to discover for himself the countless ways in which non-harmonic tones can be used effectively. This study should consist of playing the chorales at the piano, participating in small groups to sing the chorales, and constant analysis of the technical means used to achieve the musical and artistic results.

APPLICATION

WRITTEN MATERIALS

Any non-harmonic tone can be included in a harmonic progression through use of the following rule.

Part-Writing Rule 8. When a non-harmonic tone is used, the non-harmonic tone temporarily replaces a harmonic tone. Write the triad with normal doubling, if possible, and substitute the non-harmonic tone for one of the triad tones. Introduce and leave the non-harmonic tone according to the definition of the particular tone being used.

Application of this rule has been demonstrated several times in this chapter (Figures 19.2, 19.3, 19.4, and so on). Similar application can be made to any of the other musical illustrations.

In writing non-harmonic tones, particular care should be taken with any non-harmonic tone located at the interval of a seventh above the root of a chord. Such a tone creates the aural effect of a seventh chord, even when of short duration. Therefore, it always proceeds downwards. Review Chapter 7, pages 73-74.

Assignment 95. Writing passing tones and neighboring tones. Fill in alto and tenor voices. Make harmonic analysis. Circle each non-harmonic tone and identify it.

Assignment 96. Writing suspensions (passing tones and neighboring tones will also be found in this assignment). Fill in alto and tenor voices. Make harmonic analysis. Circle each non-harmonic tone and identify it.

Sections 1-4: 9 8, 7 6, 4 3 and $\frac{5}{2}$ suspensions

Section   5: 9 suspension; chain suspensions, plus above

Sections 6-7: ornamental suspensions, plus above

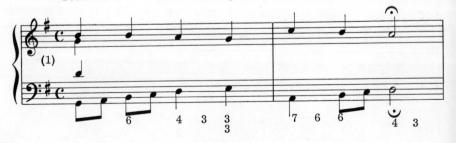

Assignment 97. Writing anticipations, appoggiaturas and escaped tones (all previous non-harmonic tones will also be included). Fill in alto and tenor voices. Make harmonic analysis. Circle each non-harmonic tone and identify it.

Assignment 98. Writing multiple non-harmonic tones. Fill in alto and tenor voices. Make harmonic analysis. Circle and identify each non-harmonic tone.

Melody Harmonization Using Non-Harmonic Tones

In four-part vocal style, non-harmonic tones may be used very sparingly, as in a simple church hymn where perhaps only a single passing tone is found at the final cadence. At the other extreme, they may be used to make each of the four vocal parts a truly melodic line, as in the chorales of Johann Sebastian Bach. In these chorales the use of non-harmonic tones allows almost continual melodic movement from one chord to the next, in contrast to the "block chord" effect of the usual church hymn.

The use of non-harmonic tones to create the effect of continual melodic movement can be supplemented by two other devices.

a) By changing the structure of the chord, or by changing the inversion of the chord on the weak half of the beat (for example, on the second eighth note when a quarter note receives one beat).

Fig. 19.33.   Bach, *O Gott, du frommer Gott* (#337)

b) By changing chords within the beat duration.

Fig. 19.34.   Bach, *Alles ist an Gottes Segen* (#128)

When harmonizing a melody line, care must be exercised not to create parallel fifths and octaves through the use of non-harmonic tones.

Fig. 19.35.

Assignment 99. Music examples in four voice parts are furnished. Add passing tones at appropriate places. Any given note may be placed on the weak half of the beat to make a place for an accented passing tone.

Assignment 100. Add suspensions and passing tones to the examples given. Given notes may be changed rhythmically to make suspensions possible.

Assignment 101. Harmonize melodies from Assignment 86 using non-harmonic tones.

Assignment 102. Write original exercises showing the use of various non-harmonic tones, as assigned.

EAR TRAINING AND MUSIC READING

Sight Singing. The use of the altered non-harmonic tone in the melodic line is presented in Chapters 8b and 13b of *Music for Sight Singing*. The melodies in these chapters also contain a few examples of notes altered because of an altered chord.

Exercise 111. Melodic dictation. Melodies containing altered non-harmonic tones will now be given in dictation. Be sure to spell the non-harmonic tone according to the direction in which it resolves.

Exercise 112. Harmonic dictation exercises will now contain non-harmonic tones.

Unaccented non-harmonic tones: Since these sound after the chord has sounded, the harmony may be identified before the movement to the non-harmonic tone.

Accented non-harmonic tones: These sound simultaneously with the chord. The pure chord sound will be heard at the resolution of the non-harmonic tone.

Dictation may now include all four voices. After taking down the chord numbers, listen to each voice as a melodic line when the exercise is played.

Self-Help in Harmonic Dictation

Sicilian Mariner's Hymn	1-2	M-26,E-247	Helmsley	(all)	E-5
Wareham	1-4	M-38	St. Stephen	5-8	E-11
St. Magnus	5-8	M-78	Isleworth	1-2	E-77
Waits' Carol	1-8	M-103	Richter	1-2	E-154
Aberystwyth	1-2	M-338,E-415	Vetter	5-8	E-160
Dessau	1-2	M-390	Schmuecke dich	1-3	E-210

Meyer   5-8 M-425

Bremen   1-4 M-534   Jesus, Lord, Be
                                       Thou Mine Own 1-4 G-44

                                       Loving Shepherd
                                               1-4, 7-8 G-45

                                       As Fades the
                                       Glowing Orb   1-2 G-139

KEYBOARD HARMONY

Exercise 113. Play examples from Assignments 95-97 at the keyboard.

Introduction to
Diatonic Seventh Chords;
Rhythm: Syncopation

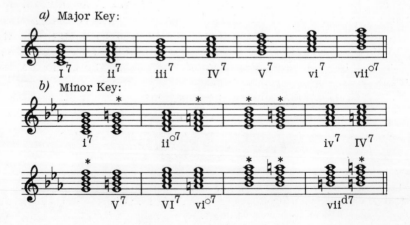

THEORY AND ANALYSIS

A seventh chord consists of a triad plus the interval of a seventh above the root of the triad (review pages 71-72). Seventh chords may be built upon any scale degree. Figure 20.1 shows all possible diatonic seventh chords. Included are those seventh chords in a minor key which utilize the raised sixth and seventh scale steps of the melodic minor scale. Chords marked * are infrequently or rarely used.

Fig. 20.1.

Seventh chords may be described by the quality of their sound.
a) The triad comprising the root, third and fifth will be identified by the usual terms: major, minor and diminished.
b) The interval between the root and the seventh of the chord
will be identified according to its size (see Chapter 1:14, *Intervals*).

Examples:

1) major-minor seventh chord: *major* triad plus *minor* seventh.
G B D F: G B D = *major* triad; G up to F = *minor* seventh; G B D F
is a major-minor seventh chord.

2) major-major seventh chord: major triad plus major seventh.
C E G B: C E G = *major* triad; C up to B = *major* seventh; C E G B
is a major-major seventh chord (for simplicity, the term *major
seventh chord* may be used).

3) minor-minor seventh chord: minor triad plus *minor* seventh.
D F A C: D F A = *minor* triad; D up to C = *minor* seventh: D F A C =
minor-minor seventh chord (for simplicity, the term *minor seventh
chord* may be used).

4) diminished-minor seventh chord: *diminished* triad plus *minor*
seventh. D F A$\flat$ C: D F A$\flat$ = *diminished* triad; D up to C = *minor*
seventh; D F A$\flat$ C = diminished minor seventh chord (this chord is
also known as a *half diminished seventh chord*.)

5) diminished-diminished seventh chord: diminished triad plus *diminished* seventh. B D F A$\flat$: B D F = *diminished* triad; B up to A$\flat$ =
diminished seventh; B D F A$^\flat$ = diminished-diminished seventh
chord (for simplicity, the term *diminished seventh chord* may be
used.)

Roman numeral designations for seventh chords are as follows:
a) The Roman numeral will indicate the type of triad found as
root, third and fifth of the seventh chord, except in diminished
seventh chords—see *b)* below.

b) The superscript ^{7} indicates the presence of an interval of a
seventh above the root of the chord. This seventh above the root will
be diatonic in the key. The superscript ^{d7} indicates that *both* the
triad and the interval of the seventh are diminished; the Roman numeral in this case indicates simply the scale step on which the
chord is built.[1]

Examples of Roman numeral designations

C major or minor V^7: V = G B D; ^{7} = F; V^7 = G B D F

C major ii^7: ii = D F A; ^{7} = C; ii^7 = D F A C

---

[1]This exception is made in the interest of the simplification of symbols,
particularly for those altered chords which are found as diminished seventh
chords. See Ottman, *Advanced Harmony: Theory and Practice* (Englewood
Cliffs, N.J.: Prentice-Hall, Inc., 1961), Chapters 6 and 9.

C minor $\qquad$ ii^{o7}: ii^o = D F A$\flat$; ^{7} = C; ii^{o7} = D F A$\flat$ C

C minor $\qquad$ vii^{d7}: diminished seventh chord built on the seventh scale step, B D F A$\flat$

C major $\qquad$ vii^{o7}: vii^o = B D F; ^{7} = A; vii^{o7} = B D F A

Figured bass symbols for seventh chords:

Root in bass: 7, usually reduced to 7 only unless 5 and 3 are altered.
  5
  3

First inversion: 6, usually reduced to 6 only.
  5   5
  3

Second inversion: 6, usually reduced to 4 only.
  4   3
  3

Third inversion: 6, usually reduced to either 4 or 2.
  4   2
  2

Fig. 20.2.

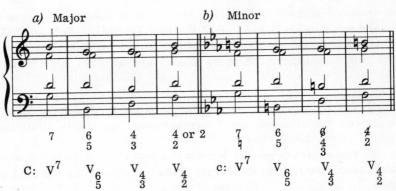

To indicate inversion in the Roman numeral designation, figured bass symbols without chromatic signs will be used as in Figure 20.2.

The treatment of the seventh of the seventh chord has much in common with the treatment of the non-harmonic tone. Both are dissonant; both must be carefully approached and resolved. In actual seventh chord usage, the three-note figure, consisting of approach, dissonance, and resolution, is similar to certain non-harmonic tone figures. In each case, the seventh resolves down by step.

Fig. 20.3.

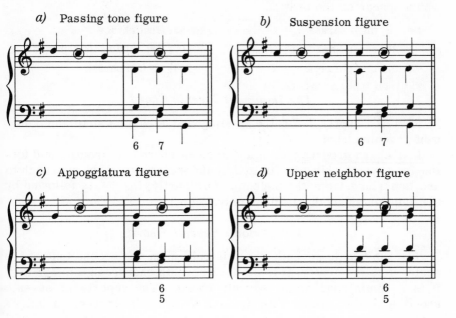

a) Passing tone figure   b) Suspension figure

c) Appoggiatura figure   d) Upper neighbor figure

Assignment 103. Identify seventh chords from Bach chorales.

a) Spell chord from root

b) Identify type of chord

c) Indicate method of approach to and departure from the seventh

Fig. 20.4.   Bach, *Puer natus in Bethlehem* (#12)

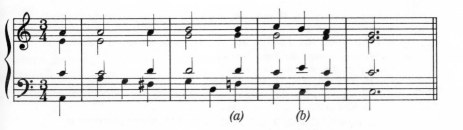

(a) G B D F—major-minor seventh chord;
seventh (F) approached by leap from below
(appoggiatura) and resolves down by step.

(b) C E G B—major seventh chord;
seventh (B) approached by step from above
(passing tone) and resolves down by step.

Do the same with these chorale phrases (analyze only those sevenths which appear on the beat).

No. 8, third phrase   93, first phrase

    24, second and last phrases   105, first and second phrases

    67, last phrase   204, second phrase

The Dominant Seventh Chord

Review Chapter 7 for the spelling and melodic use of the dominant seventh chord.

In a chord progression, the choice of chords to precede and follow the seventh chord is limited by the strictness of the approach to and departure from the seventh. Ordinarily, the V^7 is followed by the tonic or submediant triads only.

The Supertonic Seventh Chord

The supertonic seventh chord is built upon the second tone of the scale. In a major key, it is a minor seventh chord. In a minor key, it is a diminished-minor seventh chord. The supertonic seventh chord with the raised fifth (raised sixth scale degree), a minor seventh chord is theoretically possible; it is rarely used[2] and will not be considered here.

The supertonic seventh chord is found most frequently in first inversion, though it can be used with any note in the bass. It is usually followed by the dominant (V or V^7) or the tonic six-four chord.

Assignment 104. Spell the supertonic seventh in each major and minor key.

Assignment 105. Harmonic analysis. Indicate chord numbers and non-harmonic tones from the following excerpts.

Beethoven, Sonata for Piano, No. 3 (Op. 2, No. 3), first movement, measures 5-8
Chopin, Mazurka No. 18 (Op. 30, No. 1), measures 5-8 (G minor)
Mendelssohn, *Songs Without Words*
   No. 6 (Op. 19, No. 6), measures 28-29
   No. 16 (Op. 38, No. 4), measures 4-5
   No. 41 (Op. 85, No. 5), measures 6-9
   No. 43 (Op. 102, No. 1), measures 25-26
Mozart, Sonata for Piano in D Major, K. 311, third movement, measures 23-26
Schumann, *Album for the Young,* Op. 68
   No. 19, measures 17-20
   No. 28, measures 1-4
Murphy and Melcher, *Music for Study,* Chapter 15

---

[2]When the fifth of the chord (raised sixth scale degree) resolves upwards, and the seventh of the chord resolves downwards, both meet on the same note, resulting in a doubled leading tone.

APPLICATION

WRITTEN MATERIALS

Part-writing the seventh of the seventh chord. In *all* seventh chords, the seventh, being a dissonance, must be treated carefully. Part-writing Rule 9 will suffice in most instances; certain exceptions to the usual resolution of the seventh will be noted as individual seventh chords are presented.

Part-Writing Rule 9. The seventh of a seventh chord, its note of approach and its note of resolution comprise a three-note figure similar to certain non-harmonic tone figures: the passing tone figure, the suspension figure, the appoggiatura figure and the upper neighboring figure. The resolution of the seventh is usually down by step.

Part-writing the dominant seventh chord. Use of Rule 9 will suffice in most instances. Following are illustrations of each of the bass positions of the seventh chord, together with illustrations of a few of the more common exceptional practices.

a) Root in the bass. The dominant seventh chord with its root in the bass may be found complete (all four chord tones present) or incomplete (fifth missing and root doubled). The complete V^7 is often followed by an incomplete tonic triad, the incomplete V^7 by a complete tonic triad.

Fig. 20.5. Incomplete V^7 Schumann,*Das Schifflein*, Op. 146, No. 5

Fig. 20.6. Complete V^7 Beethoven, *Eligischer Gesang*, Op. 118

Following the V^7 the vi triad is usually found with a doubled third.

Fig. 20.7.   Bach, *O Herre Gott, dein göttlich Wort* (#14)

b) The V^7 in inversion.   Figures 20.8 and 20.9 show examples of all three inversions of the V^7. Note particularly

(1) The seventh of the V^7 usually descends stepwise.

(2) When the bass note of the V^7 in inversion is approached by leap, it resolves stepwise in a direction opposite to the leap, in accordance with good melodic practice.

(3) The V^7 in inversion is usually complete.

Fig. 20.8.   Hymn: Greenland

Fig. 20.9.   Hymn: Dix

In common with any other theoretical device used in music composition, many exceptions can be found in the use of the V^7. Among the more usual are

a) The passing V_4^3. This chord is found between two positions
of the tonic triad, similar to the passing V_6^4 (see Figure 20.8). When
used with an ascending bass line, the seventh of the V^7 ascends.

Fig. 20.10.   Hymn: Duke Street

b) Transfer of seventh. The V^7 may be repeated with the
seventh occurring in a different voice part. The seventh in the last
of such a series resolves normally.

Fig. 20.11.   Weber, *Mass in G*

c) Ornamental resolution of the seventh. Occasionally, the
seventh may be found ornamented, as in the ornamental resolution
of the suspension. (See also chorale 65, last phrase.)

Fig. 20.12.   Bach, *Wenn wir in höchsten Nöten sein* (#247)

d) V⁷ with an accented non-harmonic tone.

Fig. 20.13.   Beethoven, Sonata in D Major for Piano,
                                               Op. 10, No. 3

Assignment 106. Part-write dominant seventh chords with root in bass.

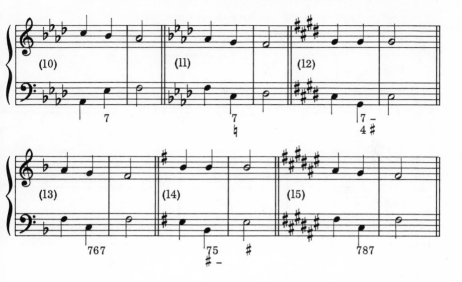

Assignment 107. Part-write dominant seventh chords in inversion.

Part-writing the supertonic seventh chord. Use of Rule 9 will take care of most situations involving the supertonic seventh. The approach to the seventh as a suspension figure is by far the most commonly used. A passing tone approach is shown in Figure 20.16. The supertonic seventh (like the supertonic triad) is most commonly found in first inversion. Only infrequently is the supertonic seventh chord found incomplete.

   a) First inversion.[3]

Fig. 20.14.   Hymn: Hesperus

---

[3]The ii$_6^5$ is sometimes considered a IV triad with added sixth (F major: B♭ D F plus G).

b) Root in bass.

Fig. 20.15.   Haydn, Mass in B♭ Major

Fig. 20.16.   Bach, *Von Gott will ich nicht lassen* (#191)

c) Third inversion.

Fig. 20.17.   Hiller (1792)*Was sorgst du ängstlich für dein Leben*

d) The ii₆₅ in conjunction with the passing I₆₄. To the list of six-four chord usages described in Chapter 18 may be added the progression IV₆ - I₆₄ - ii₆₅ (also, in minor, iv₆ - i₆₄ - ii°₆₅). This progression can be found in Figure 17.6.

e) Delayed resolution of the seventh. Occasionally the seventh of the ii⁷ is held over into the next chord. In Figure 20.16, the seventh of the ii⁷ becomes the root of the I₆, finally resolving down normally.

In Figure 20.18, the seventh of the ii^7 becomes a 4 3 suspension in the dominant triad.

Fig. 20.18.   Bach, *Wach' auf, mein Herz* (#93)

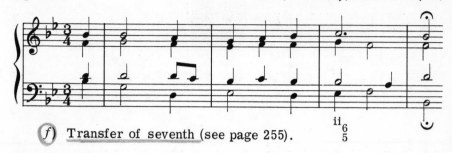

f) Transfer of seventh (see page 255). ii^6_5

Fig. 20.19.   Mozart, *Coronation Mass*, K. 317

Adagio

ii^6_5

Melody Harmonization Using Seventh Chords

A seventh chord can be used at almost any place in a musical composition where a triad built on the same scale degree can be used. However, because of the necessity of resolving the seventh, there is very little choice in the chord which follows the seventh chord. It is best to use a chord with its root a fifth below that of the seventh chord—V^7 - I; ii^7 - V. The progression V^7 - vi is also common.

In the melodic line, the fourth scale step can be harmonized as the seventh of the V^7, provided that this melody note moves down (see Figures 20.8, 20.9, 20.17). Similarly, the tonic note can be harmonized as the seventh of the ii^7 (see Figure 20.16).

Seventh chords should be used sparingly in a harmonization for the following reasons.

a) The seventh chord sound is effective because of its contrast with a triad sound. This effectiveness is lost when the seventh chord is used too often.

b) The necessity of resolving the seventh limits the choice of the following chord.

c) Non-harmonic tones are often impossible or ineffectual at those points where seventh chords are used.

Assignment 108. Part-write examples of the supertonic seventh chord.

Assignment 109. Part-write extended exercises, using both the dominant seventh and the supertonic seventh chords. Be sure that the seventh of the chord is approached and resolved correctly. Make harmonic analysis.

Assignment 110. Melody harmonization. Harmonize melodies below, using dominant seventh and supertonic seventh chords. Be sure that the seventh of the seventh chord is approached and resolved correctly. Use non-harmonic tones where appropriate. Make harmonic analysis.

(6)

Assignment 111. See "Syncopation," page 265. Write melodies in forms, as assigned, using syncopation patterns from page 265, or other patterns as found in Chapters 10 and 15 of *Music for Sight Singing.*

EAR TRAINING AND MUSIC READING

Exercise 114. Sing the progression I ii^7 V I or i ii^{o7} V i with letter names in each major or minor key.

Exercise 115. Harmonic dictation exercises will now include examples of the dominant seventh and supertonic seventh chords.

Self-Help in Harmonic Dictation

V^7

Lyons	1-8	M-4, E-260	St. Peter	1-4	M-424, E-455
Fowler	1-2	M-9	Claudius	9-12	E-138
Worship	7-8	M-10	Wigan	1-4	E-338
Irish	8-14	M-14, E-444	Sleep Holy Babe	1-4	G-14
Salzburg	1-7	M-383	Great St. Joseph	1-4	G-93
Munich	1-4	M-386, E-114			
Arlington	1-8	M-399, E-325			

ii^7 or ii^{o7}

Silver Street	11-13	M-22	St. Phillip	9-12	E-57
Ellers	9-16	M-29	Swedish Litany	1-2	E-82
Old 134th	1-4	M-39	Winkworth	1-2	E-226
Keble	1-2	M-62	Capetown	1-4	E-275
Rotterdam	1-2	M-159	Leoni	5-8	E-286
Morecambe	1-4	M-179	All Glory	1-4	G-26
Tantum Ergo	1-4	M-319	Lift Up	1-4	G-32
Spohr	1-8	M-366	Hail Holy Queen	1-8	G-83
Luther	1-4	M-385			
Bethlehem	13-16	M-552			

Syncopation

Syncopation occurs when the normal or expected pattern of rhythm, accent, or meter is deliberately upset. This effect is frequently created by tying a weak beat or a weak part of a beat into the next strong beat or part of a beat. The following are some of the basic patterns of syncopation.

Pattern	Example in *Music for Sight Singing,*
	I – 244
	I – 245
	I – 249
	II – 141
	II – 144
	I – 248
	I – 260

Syncopation may also be created by accenting a weak beat or part of a beat when there is no tie into the next strong beat or part of a beat.

Pattern	Example in *Music for Sight Singing,*
	II – 135
	I – 267
	II – 152

Exercise 116. Using the conductor's beat and background, read patterns of syncopation above. Repeat each pattern as many times as necessary.

Exercise 117. Rhythmic reading. Read rhythmically melodies from Chapters 10 and 15 of *Music for Sight Singing.*

Exercise 118. Rhythmic dictation exercises will now contain examples of syncopation.

Sight Singing. Sing melodies from Chapters 10 and 15 of *Music for Sight Singing.* (The following melodies contain examples of modulation and may be deferred at this time: I - 261, 264; II - 136, 137.)

KEYBOARD HARMONY

Exercise 119. Keyboard harmony. Play the following progressions in any major or minor key (other soprano positions may be used).

a) I (third in soprano)   - V^7 - I

b) I (root in soprano)   - $V_{\substack{6 \\ 5}}$ - I

c) IV (third in soprano) - $V_{\substack{4 \\ 2}}$ - I_6

d) vi (third in soprano) - V^7 - I

Exercise 120. Keyboard harmony. Play the following progressions at the keyboard in any major or minor key (other soprano positions may be used).

a) I (third in soprano) - $ii_{\substack{6 \\ 5}}$ - V - I

b) I (third in soprano) - $ii_{\substack{4 \\ 2}}$ - $V_{\substack{6 \\ 5}}$ - I

c) I (third in soprano) - IV_6 - $I_{\substack{6 \\ 4}}$ - $ii_{\substack{6 \\ 5}}$ - V - I   (passing tonic six-four)

Exercise 121. Melody harmonization. The progression $ii_{\substack{6 \\ 5}}$ - V - I is a very effective cadence formula.

Fig. 20.20.

Harmonize the following melodies at the keyboard, using the cadence formula ii$_6^5$ - V - I—*Music for Sight Singing,* Part I - 11, 108, 123, 182; Part II - 19, 24, 74, 81.

Appendix 1

The Essentials of Part-Writing

THE SINGLE CHORD

APPROXIMATE RANGE OF THE FOUR VOICES

Soprano: d^1 - g^2 Alto: a - c^2

Tenor: f - f^1 Bass: F - c^1

TRIAD POSITION

In *open position,* the distance between the soprano and tenor is an octave or more. In *close position,* the distance between the soprano and tenor is less than an octave. The distance between adjacent voices normally does not exceed an octave, although more than an octave may appear between bass and tenor.

NORMAL DOUBLING

Diatonic major and minor triads

a) root in bass: double the root
b) first inversion: double the soprano note
c) second inversion: double the bass note
d) exception, minor triads, root or third in bass: the third of a minor triad is often doubled, particularly when this third is the tonic, subdominant or dominant note of the key.

Diminished triad (usually found in first inversion only): double the third; when the fifth is in the soprano, the fifth is usually doubled.

Augmented triad: double the bass note

268

Seventh chord: normally, all four voices are present. In the major-minor seventh chord, the root is often doubled and the fifth omitted.

Altered triad: normally, same doubling as non-altered triads; avoid doubling the altered note.

CHORD CONNECTION

TRIAD ROOTS

When the bass tones of two successive triads are the *roots* of the triads

Triad roots are repeated

Rule 1.   Both triads may be written in the same position, or each may be in different position. Triad positions should be changed

   a) when necessary to keep voices in correct pitch range

   b) when necessary to keep correct voice distribution (two roots, one third and one fifth).

   c) to avoid large leaps in an inner part

Triad roots are a fifth apart

Rule 2A.   Retain the common tone; move the other voice stepwise.

Rule 2B.   Move the three upper voices in similar motion to the nearest tones of the next triad.

Rule 2C.   (Exception) The third of the first chord moves to the third of the second chord; hold the common tone and the other voice moves stepwise.

Rule 2D.   (Exception) At the cadence, the root of the final tonic triad may be tripled, omitting the fifth.

Triad roots are a second apart

Rule 3.   The three upper voices move contrary to the bass.

Triad roots are a third apart

Rule 4A.   Hold the two common tones; the other voice moves stepwise.

Rule 4B.   The three upper voices move contrary to the bass.

Exception

Rule 5.   When it is impossible to follow Rules 2, 3 and 4, without incurring parallel fifths and octaves or augmented seconds, double the third in the second of the two triads.

TRIADS IN INVERSION

Progression to or from a triad in *inversion,* a triad with a *doubled third,* or a triad with any *unusual doubling*

Rule 6A. Write the two voices moving to or from the doubled note first, using oblique or contrary motion if possible.

Rule 6B. When first inversions of triads are found in succession, each triad must have a different doubling to avoid parallel octaves, or the same doubling may appear in different pairs of voices. Avoid doubling the leading tone or any altered tone. Approach and leave each doubled tone using Rule 6A.

POSITION CHANGES

Rule 7. Triad position may be changed
a) at a repeated triad.
b) using Rule 2C.
c) at a triad in inversion or a triad with unusual doubling, following Rule 6A.

NON-HARMONIC TONES

Rule 8. A non-harmonic tone temporarily replaces a harmonic tone. Write the triad with normal doubling if possible and substitute the non-harmonic tone for one of the chord tones. Approach and leave the non-harmonic tone according to the definition of the non-harmonic tone being used.

SEVENTH CHORDS

Rule 9. The seventh of a seventh chord, its note of approach and its note of resolution comprise a three-note figure similar to certain non-harmonic tone figures: passing tone, suspension, appoggiatura and upper neighbor. The seventh usually resolves down by step.

ALTERED CHORDS

Rule 10. Use of altered chords does not change part-writing procedure. Do not double altered note. Follow Rule 6A if unusual doubling occurs.

GENERAL RULE

Rule 11. In situations not covered by Rules 1-10, observe the following:
a) Move each voice the shortest distance possible.
b) Move the soprano and bass in contrary or oblique motion if possible.

c) Avoid doubling the leading tone, any altered note, any non-harmonic tone or the seventh of a seventh chord.

d) Avoid parallel fifths, parallel octaves and the melodic interval of the augmented second.

Appendix 2

Instrumentation: Ranges, Clefs, Transposition

Range

The range given for each instrument is approximately that ordinarily used by the average player. Neither the lowest nor the highest note playable by the instrument is necessarily included. These ranges will be found satisfactory for purposes of this text.

Clef

Each instrument regularly uses the clef or clefs found in the musical illustrations under "Range." Exceptions or modifying statements are found under the heading "Clef."

Transposition

Unless other wise indicated under this heading, pitches given under "Range" sound concert pitch when played. (Concert pitch: A^1 = 440 vibrations per second; the note A^1 on the piano keyboard is concert A). All transposing instruments sound their name when written C is played; for example, a Clarinet in $B^\flat$ sounds $B^\flat$ when it plays a written C.

STRING INSTRUMENTS

VIOLIN

Range

VIOLA

Range

Clef. Alto clef is used almost exclusively. Treble clef is used occasionally for sustained high passages.

VIOLONCELLO ('CELLO)

Range

Clef. Bass clef is ordinarily used. Tenor clef is used for extended passages above small A. Treble clef is used for extreme upper range (not shown).

DOUBLE-BASS (BASS-VIOL, CONTRABASS)

Range

Transposition. Notes sound an octave lower than written.

WOODWIND INSTRUMENTS

FLUTE

Range

OBOE

Range

CLARINET: B♭ and A

Range

Transposition

a) Clarinet in B♭. Notes sound a major second lower than written. Use signature for the key a major second *above* concert pitch.

b) Clarinet in A. Notes sound a minor third lower than written. Use signature for the key a minor third above concert pitch.

BASSOON

Range

Clef.   Bass clef is ordinarily used.   Tenor clef is used for upper range.

ENGLISH HORN (COR ANGLAIS)

Range

Transposition.   Notes sound a perfect fifth lower than written. Use signature for the key a perfect fifth *above* concert pitch.

HORN (FRENCH HORN)

Range

Clef.   Treble clef is commonly used.
Transposition.   Notes sound a perfect fifth lower than written. Key signatures are not ordinarily used. Write in all accidentals. In many published horn parts, notes written in the bass clef sound a perfect fourth higher than written. Consult with player of instrument before writing horn part in bass clef.

Horn parts are occasionally written in D and E♭.

SAXOPHONES: E♭ Alto, B♭ Tenor and E♭ Baritone

Range

Transposition

a) E♭ Alto Saxophone. Notes sound a major sixth lower than written. Use signature for the key a major sixth *above* concert pitch.

b) B♭ Tenor Saxophone. Notes sound a major ninth (an octave plus a major second) lower than written. Use signature for the key a major second *above* concert pitch.

c) E♭ Baritone Saxophone. Notes sound an octave plus a major sixth lower than written. Use signature for the key a major sixth *above* concert pitch.

BRASS INSTRUMENTS

TRUMPET OR CORNET, B♭ and C

Range

Transposition

a) Trumpet or Cornet in B♭. Notes sound a major second lower than written. Use signature for the key a major second *above* concert pitch.

b) Trumpet or Cornet in C. Non-transposing—sounds as written.

TROMBONE

Range

Clef.   Both tenor and bass clefs are commonly used.

TUBA

Range

Index

A

Accented cadential six-four chord, 107, 113, 210
Accented passing tone, 128
Accessory tone, 133
Accidental, 16
Accompaniment figures, 145
Added sixth, 258
Alla breve, 12
Altered music, 15
Alto clef, 81
Anonymous, *Nun sich der Tag geendet hat*, 85
Antecedent phrase, 41
Anticipation, 130
  double, 230
Anti-climax note, 46
Appoggiatura, 130, 133
  double, 230
  triple, 230
Appoggiatura chord, 232
Appoggiatura figure in seventh chord, 251
Arpeggiated six-four chord, 211
Augmented fourth:
  in dominant seventh chord, 72
  in diminished triad, 149
  in part-writing, 116
Augmented intervals, 5
Augmented prime, 5
Augmented second, 5
  melodic use, 92
Augmented sixth, 5
Augmented triad, 8

Authentic cadences, 69
Auxiliary tone, 133

B

Bach, J.S., chorales, 70, 71, 85, 87, 93, 96, 112, 125-130, 135, 136, 141, 149, 151, 152, 154, 157, 165, 166, 168, 188, 190-192, 195, 208, 211, 224-232, 235, 243, 244, 251, 254, 255, 259, 260
Bach, K.P.E., *Der Tag des Weltgerichts*, 180
Baritone clef, 83
Bar, 10
Bar-line, 10
Bass suspension, 225
Beam, 13
Beat, 10, 27
  compound, 29
  conductor's, 36
  divided, 29
  simple, 29
  subdivided, 122
Beethoven, Ludwig van:
  Eligischer Gesang, 253
  Quartet, Op. 18, No. 1, 82
  Sonata for Piano, Op. 2, No. 2, 233
  Sonata for Piano, Op. 10, No. 3, 256

Beethoven, Ludwig van (cont.)
Symphony No. 3, 142
Brahms, Johannes:
Gypsy Songs, 232
Sankt Raphael, 209
Schnitter Tod, 208
Vergebliches Ständchen, 183
Die Wollust in den Maien, 95
Bytones, 133

C

Cadence:
authentic:
half, 69
imperfect, 69
perfect, 69
deceptive, 187
definition, 21
evasion, 179
half:
authentic, 69
Phrygian, 209
plagal, 87
ii-V, 209
IV-V, 209
VI-V, 209
Phrygian, 209
plagal:
half, 87
imperfect, 87
perfect, 86
Cadential six-four chord, 107, 113, 210
C clef, 81
Chain suspension, 227
Changing tone, 131, 133
Chopin, Frédéric:
Waltz, Op. 64, No. 2, 235
Waltz, Op. 69, No. 1, 236
Chord, 8
broken, 8
Chord progression:
I, IV, and V, 139
ii, 173
iii, 203
vi, 203
vii°, 159
special use of tonic, 191
Chord symbols:
seventh chords:
inversion, 250

root in bass, 248
triads:
inversion, 106
root in bass, 15
Chromatics, 2
placement, 13
Chromatic scale, 5
Circle of keys, 8
Clef:
alto, 81
bass, 1
C, 81
F, 1
G, 1
instrumental use, 118, 272
tenor, 81
transposition by, 84
treble, 1
Climax note, 46
Close position, 51
Close structure, 51
Common time, 11
Compound time, 31
Concert pitch, 272
Conductor's beat, 36
Consequent phrase, 41
Consonant triad, 149
Contrasting period, 41
Crüger, Johann, *Herzliebster Jesu*, 73
Cut time, 11

D

Deceptive cadence, 187
Diatonic music, 15
Diminished fifth:
in diminished triad, 149
in dominant seventh chord, 72
Diminished intervals, 5-6
Diminished-minor seventh chord, 249
Diminished seventh chord, 249
Diminished triad, 8, 149
Direct fifth, 158
Direct octave, 158
Dissonant triad, 149
Distance between voices, 52
Dominant seventh chord, 71, 252, 253
Dominant tone, 5
Dominant triad, 68
Dotted note, 10
placement on staff, 12

Double anticipation, 230
Double appoggiatura, 230
Double bar, 10
Double flat, 2
Double neighboring tone, 229
Double passing tone, 228
Double period, 181
Double suspension, 229
Double sharp, 2
Doubling:
  diminished triad, 152
  dominant seventh chord, 254
  major triad, 51
  minor triad, 166
  Phrygian cadence, 212
Down-beat, 36
Dvořák, Antonin, Concerto for Violoncello and Orchestra, 82

double period, 181
extension, 178
motive, 41
period, 41
phrase, 41
phrase group, 180
Foster, Stephen, *Old Folks at Home,*
  142
French violin clef, 83

E

Échappée, 130
Escaped tone, 130
Evasion of cadence, 178
Extension of phrase, 178

F

Feminine beginning, ending, 43
Fifths:
  direct, 158
  hidden, 158
  parallel, 92
  unequal, 154
Figured bass:
  definition, 61
  non-harmonic tones, 222
  seventh chords, 250
  triads:
    first inversion, 105
    root in bass, 61
    second inversion, 106
First inversion:
  seventh chord, 250
  triad, 105
Flat, 2
Foreign tone, 133
Form:
  definition, 41

G

Grace note, 134
Graun, Carl Heinrich, *Der Tod Jesu,*
  187

H

Half cadence:
  authentic, 69
  Phrygian, 209
  plagal, 87
  ii-V, IV-V, VI-V, 209
Half diminished seventh chord, 249
Half step, 2
Handel, George Frederick, *Messiah,*
  108
Harmonic dictation:
  basic procedures, 78, 103, 119
  definition, 78
  self-help procedures, 119
Harmonic rhythm, 141, 173
Haydn, Franz Joseph:
  Canon, 80
  The Creation, 134
  Mass in B♭ Major, 259
  Missa Sanctae Caecilae, 224
  Sonata in D for Piano, 165
  Symphony in G Major, No. 100, 177,
    182
Hidden fifth, 158
Hidden octave, 158
Hiller, Johann Adam, *Was sorgst du
  ängstlich für dein Leben,* 259
Hindemith, Paul, String Trio, Op. 34,
  32
Hymn tune names, 86

I

Inner pedal, 131
Instrumental range, 118, 272
Instrumentation, 118, 272
Internal pedal, 131
Interval:
  augmented, 6
  definition, 5-6
  diminished, 5-6
  in diminished triad, 149
  in dominant seventh chord, 72
  enharmonic, 5-6
  harmonic, 24
  inversion, 6
  major, 5-6
  in major triad, 17
  melodic, 24
  minor, 5-6
  in minor triad, 58
  perfect, 5-6
  sight singing, 184
Inversion:
  intervals, 6
  seventh chords, 250
  triads, 105
Inverted pedal, 131

K

Key, 6-7
Keyboard:
  accompaniment figures, 145
  key names, 3
  melody harmonization, 144 ff.
  scale harmonization, 206
Keys:
  circle of, 8
  enharmonic, 8
  parallel, 8
  relative, 7
Key signature:
  definition, 6
  major keys, 7
  minor keys, 7

L

Leading tone, 4-5

in melodic line, 46
Leading tone triad, 148
Leger (ledger) lines, 2
  placement, 12
Liber Usualis, 21

M

Major-minor seventh chord, 249
Major second, 5
Major seventh, 6
Major seventh chord, 250
Major sixth, 6
  in dominant seventh chord, 72
  in major triad, 17
  in minor triad, 58
Major third, 6
  in dominant seventh chord, 72
  in major triad, 17
  in minor triad, 58
Major triad, 8, 15
Masculine beginning, ending, 43
Mason, Lowell, 21
Measure, 10
Mediant tone, 5
Mediant triad, 186
Melodic dictation:
  basic procedures, 47
  definition, 47
  self-help procedures, 48
Melodic line:
  characteristics, 40
  harmonic background, 138
Melodic memory, 39
Melody harmonization:
  basic procedures, 101, 156
  keyboard, 144 ff.
Memory, melodic, 39
Mendelssohn, Felix:
  Christus, 189
  Das Schifflein, 180
  Elijah, 194
  St. Paul, 194
  Venetianisches Gondellied, 181
Meter, 29
Meter signature, 30 (see also Time
  signatures)
Metronome, 10, 11, 27
Mezzo-soprano clef, 83
Minor dominant triad, 208
Minor second, 5
Minor seventh, 6

Minor seventh (cont.)
  in dominant seventh chord, 72
Minor seventh chord, 249
Minor sixth, 6
  in major triad, 17
  in minor triad, 59
Minor third, 5
  in dominant seventh chord, 72
  in major triad, 17
  in minor triad, 58
Minor triad, 8, 58
M. M., 10
Mode, 209
Motion between soprano and bass, 157
Motive, 41
Mozart, Wolfgang Amadeus:
  Concerto for Clarinet and Orchestra, 179
  Coronation Mass, K. 317, 260
  Sonata in C Major for Piano, K. 279, 137
  Sonata in D Major for Piano, K. 284, 150
  Sonata in F Major for Piano, K. 332, 233
Music reading *(see* Rhythm, Sight singing)

N

Natural, 2, 13
Neighboring tone, 129
  double, 229
Neighboring tone figure in seventh chord, 251
Non-chord tone, 133
Non-harmonic tone:
  ambiguous, 227
  chromatic, 233
  definitions, 127-131
  multiple, 228
  table of, 132
  terminology variants, 133
  use in seventh chords, 251
  (see also Anticipation, Appoggiatura, Changing tone, Escaped tone, Neighboring tone, Passing tone, Pedal, Retardation, and Suspension)
Notes:
  horizontal arrangement, 13

note lengths, 9
  parts of, 11-12
  placement on staff, 11-12
  relative duration, 9
  vertical arrangement, 12

O

Octave, 6
Octave registers, 3
Octaves:
  direct, 158
  hidden, 158
  parallel, 92
  stationary, 93
Open position, 51
Open structure, 51
Organ point, 131
Ornamental resolution:
  seventh chord, 255
  suspension, 226
Overlapping parts, 116

P

Parallel fifths, 92, 232
Parallel keys, 8
Parallel octaves, 92
Parallel period, 42
Part-writing:
  augmented second, 92
  augmented fourth, 116
  choral performance, 118
  definition, 49
  doubling, 51, 152, 166, 212, 253
  instrumental performance, 118
  overlapping parts, 116
  parallel motion, 92
  performance, 118
  rules, list of, 268
  rule 1, 53
  rule 2A, 75
  rule 2B, 75
  rule 2C, 94
  rule 2D, 96
  rule 3, 92
  rule 4A, 193
  rule 4B, 194
  rule 5, 168

Part-writing (cont.)
  rule 5 (cont.)
    exception, 193
  rule 6A, 111
  rule 6B, 113
  rule 7, 116
  rule 8, 236
  rule 9, 253
  triad position (structure), 51
Passing four-three chord, 255
Passing six-four chord, 210, 259
Passing tone:
  accented, 128
  definition, 127
  double, 229
  triple, 232
  unaccented, 128
Passing tone figure in seventh
  chord, 251
Pedal, 131
Pedal point, 131, 232
Period, 41
Perfect fifth, 6
  in major triad, 17
  in minor triad, 58
Perfect fourth, 6
  in major triad, 17
  in minor triad, 58
Perfect octave, 6
  in major triad, 17
  in minor triad, 58
Perfect prime, 6
Phrase, 41
  antecedent, 41
  beginnings, 43
  consequent, 41
  endings, 43
  extension, 178
  motives in, 41
  repetition, 178
Phrase group, 180
Phrygian cadence, 209
Picardy third, 70
Pitch names, 1
Plagal cadences, 86
Plainsong, 21
Preparation, 133
Primary triads, 68
Prime:
  augmented, 6
  perfect, 6

R

Range:
  instrumental, 118, 272
  vocal, 51
Ravel, Maurice, *L'enfant et les Sortilèges,* 93
Relative keys, 7
Rests, 8–9
Retardation, 129
Rhythm:
  beat, 27
  compound time, 32
  definition, 29
  divided beat, 28–29
  simple time, 30
  subdivided beat, 122
  syncopation, 265
Rhythmic dictation:
  basic procedure, 39
  definition, 38
  self-help procedures, 39
Rhythmic syllables:
  divided beat, 37
  subdivided beat, 122
Rhythmic transcription, 35
Roman numeral symbols (*see* Chord symbols)

S

Saint-Saëns, Camille, *Samson and Delilah,* 94
Scale:
  chromatic, 5
  degree names, 5
  harmonic minor, 4
  keyboard harmonization, 206
  major, 3
  melodic minor, 4
  pure (natural) minor, 4
Schein, Johann, *Ach lob den Herrn,* 192
Schubert, Franz:
  Am See, 180
  Frühlingstraum, 188
  Klage an den Mond, 143
Schumann, Robert, *Das Schifflein,* 253
Secondary triads, 148

Second inversion:
  seventh chords, 250
  triads, 105
Self-help procedures:
  harmonic dictation, 119
  melodic dictation, 48
  memory, 39
  rhythmic dictation, 39
Sequence, 45, 179
Seventh chord:
  chord symbols, 248
  definition, 71
  delayed resolution, 259
  diminished, 249
  diminished minor, 249
  dominant, 71, 252
  figured bass, 250
  half diminished, 249
  inversion, 250
  major, 249
  major-minor, 249
  minor, 249
  ornamental resolution, 255
  passing four-three, 255
  Roman numeral symbols, 248
  supertonic, 252
  transfer of seventh, 255
Sharp, 2
Sight singing:
  definition, 46
  table of intervals, 184
Simple time, 30
Six-four chord:
  arpeggiated, 211
  cadential, 107, 210
  passing, 210
  pedal, 211
Slur, 14
Soprano clef, 83
Staff, 1
  great (grand), 2
  spellings, 1
Stationary octaves, 93
Subdivided beat, 122
Subdominant tone, 5
Subdominant triad, 85
Submediant tone, 5
Submediant triad, 186
Subtonic tone, 5
Supertonic tone, 5
Supertonic triad, 164
Supertonic seventh chord, 252
Suspension, 129, 133, 223
  bass, 225
  chain, 227

double, 229
ornamental resolution, 226
2 3, 225
4 3, 224
$\frac{5}{2}$, 225
5 4, 225
7 6, 224
9, 226
9 8, 224
Suspension figure in seventh chord,
  251
Syllables, rhythmic, 37, 122
Symbols, chord *(see* Chord symbols)
Syncopation, 265

T

Tempo, 10
  in melody harmonization, 140
Tenor clef, 81
Terminology variants:
  non-harmonic tones, 133
  vii° triad, 151
  time signatures, 34
Third inversion, 250
Thorough bass, 61 *(see also* Figured
  bass)
Tie, 10
Tierce de Picardie, 70
Time signatures:
  compound, 31
  definition, 10-11
  simple, 30
  terminology variant, 34
Tonic tone, 5
Transcription, rhythmic, 35
Transposition:
  by clef, 84
  instrumental, 118, 272
Triad:
  augmented, 8
  chord symbols, 15
  consonant, 150
  definition, 8
  diminished, 8, 149
  dissonant, 150
  dominant, 68
  leading tone, 148
  major, 8, 15
    spelling, 16
  mediant, 186

Triad (cont.):
  minor, 8, 58
  minor dominant, 208
  principal, 68
  Roman numeral symbols, 15
  secondary, 148
  subdominant, 85
  submediant, 186
  supertonic, 164
  terminology, 16
Triple appoggiatura, 230
Triple passing tone, 231
Tritone, 72, 149
Tschaikowski, Peter, Symphony No. 6, 83

U

Unaccented passing tone, 128
Unequal fifths, 154

Unison, 12
Up-beat, 36

V

Verdi, Giuseppi, *Aïda,* 234
Vocal range, 51
Vulpius, Melchior, *Der Tag bricht an,* 190

W

Wagner, Richard, *Lohengrin,* 189, 211
Weber, Carl Maria, Mass in G, 255
Whole step, 2